Presented To:

_____

From:

_____

Date:

_____

WHAT ON EARTH IS GLORY?

WHAT ON EARTH IS GLORY?

a practical approach to a glory-filled life

PAUL MANWARING

DESTINY IMAGE® PUBLISHERS, INC.

P.O. Box 310, Shippensburg, PA 17257-0310

"Speaking to the Purposes of God for This Generation and for the Generations to Come."

This book and all other Destiny Image, Revival Press, MercyPlace, Fresh Bread, Destiny Image Fiction, and Treasure House books are available at Christian bookstores and distributors worldwide.

For a U.S. bookstore nearest you, call **1-800-722-6774**.

For more information on foreign distributors, call **717-532-3040**.

Reach us on the Internet: **www.destinyimage.com**.

ISBN 13 TP: 978-0-7684-3860-4

ISBN 13 Ebook: 978-0-7684-8969-9

For Worldwide Distribution, Printed in the U.S.A.

1 2 3 4 5 6 7 8 9 10 11 / 13 12 11

DEDICATION

Sue, you are the love of my life. Your courage carved a new course for our family's story, and your love shaped it.

James, my son: your sacrificial love gave me permission to be who I am, and as you continue to succeed, you bring me great joy.

Luke, my son: your unfailing ability to make me laugh in every circumstance and your "commitment to the journey" are priceless.

Amy, my daughter-in-law: I cannot imagine our family without you. You have completed James, and you are a wonderful wife, teacher, and mother to Aidan.

Douglas Edward Manwaring, my dad (10/12/21–2/28/73): you laid a foundation, and your DNA took me to management, the broken, and the pulpit.

Ruth, my mother: thank you for always believing in me and never giving up on God.

Ivor: my Jewish prison boss, who taught me about putting family first.

Pastors Bill and Kris: it is your faith and trust in me that have given me this unbelievable opportunity for glory. I am forever indebted to you both.

My daughters: you know who you are! You have encouraged me beyond words.

And to the countless leaders who have trusted and opened their hearts to me as I have traveled this new journey of "ministry."

Finally, to my heavenly Father: I can't believe this journey, but You did!

ACKNOWLEDGMENTS

From the love of my family, the church family, and senior management team at Bethel, Redding, to the hundreds of friends, colleagues, and fellow Christians around the world, I am a blessed man in the support and encouragement I have received. Special thanks to our two home groups since we have lived in Redding: the first made our move possible and the second has become our family.

Writing a book is a strange and wonderful experience, especially when it comes to grammar and spelling! Many have helped me with this, but I am indebted to Charity Reed and Chelsea Moore, who have carried the baton of day-to-day help and encouragement in this project. Thanks to Ken Williams and my Global Legacy Team, who have encouraged me and supported me and probably done more than they should in this and every other project of my life! Thanks also to my sons for my two favorite stories, "No Way!" and "I Felt Like You, Dad."

Monumental, though, is the editing of Allison Armerding. There just simply wouldn't be a book without her. You are a genius! And finally, thanks to Dann Farrelly and Pam Spinosi for your willingness to read the nearly final document and bring it to completion.

A special acknowledgement goes to my dad, Douglas Edward Manwaring (10/12/1921–2/28/1973). I have included the text of one of his sermons as Chapter 13. What an honor to enable his name to live on, for he was taken through the gates of pearl too early for this world to really know who he was!

ENDORSEMENTS

I am in mild and increasing shock over this book I have just browsed. This man has been gripped by the glory of God and thus has a grip on it to an extent I have not witnessed before. I recently heard an oral presentation of its contents and experienced firsthand its powerful impact. Now my head is spinning with excitement as I try to assess its potentially massive effect on the world in the next years for decades to come. May the reader run through it hilariously, return and walk through it slowly, and return again and again to drink from its pages.

Jack Taylor, President
Dimensions Ministries
Melbourne, Florida

This unusual book unveils the sum total of God's attributes—His glory—but shows you, in a readable and practical way, how to bring glory to God in your own life here on Earth. This book should teach you to be more like Jesus and make you want to bring more glory to Him.

R. T. Kendall
Former Minister, Westminster Chapel
London

Ever since the days of Moses, mystics have peered into the inexpressible realm of glory. Like a photographer aiming a telephoto lens at something in the distance that is difficult to make out, they tediously dial the bezel of the camera to bring it into focus. The journey of Paul Manwaring is one that brings the seemingly surreal properties of the glory of God into sharp focus. He has taken the profound elements of the glory and enabled us to grasp them for practical application. When you have read the last word of the last chapter, you will walk away not just informed, but transformed.

Randall Worley, PhD
Headwaters Ministries

It is too easy to settle for second best. We become content with trying to do better, wanting to know God more, being convinced of the truth we believe, but scared to encounter this God in living reality.

Paul Manwaring strips away the veils and calls us out of the shadows. He insists that God can be known other than by hearsay.

He demands that we seek to encounter the presence, the genuine glory, of God in the vivid Technicolor of personal experience.

Some books will broaden your opinion; some may even alter your mind: this one threatens to change your life.

If it were a matter of buying one book this year and reading it from cover to cover, then this is the one—because this book really does demand a new way of living for all who are not satisfied with second best.

Clive Calver, Senior Pastor
Walnut Hill Community Church, Bethel, Connecticut
Author of *Dying to Live*

My dear friend Paul has written a life-changing book! I wept as I received an impartation of a glorious God bringing His children to glory. My heart was burning, my mind was renewed, and my eyes were seeing clearly from

Heaven's view. The whole creation is waiting for the freedom of the glory of the Sons of God (see Rom. 8:21-22).

You are glorious because the *standard of glory is in you!* Be what you are meant to be, and do what you were created to do…that's glory!

Living life from glory, not toward it, is a Kingdom revelation that will result in a glorious transformation. Read this book! Then let it read you!

Leif Hetland
President, Global Mission Awareness
Author of *Soaring as Eagles* and *Healing the Orphan Spirit*

Often, when we think of God's glory, mystical images of a purple mist hovering over the Lord's people emerge in our minds. Paul Manwaring's book, *What on Earth Is Glory?* opens up our spirit to new dimensions of God's nature. This book is not so much a theological manuscript, a Hebrew or Greek word study, or a historic description of glory; rather, it is a revelatory account of God's majesty put on display by the daily acts of His people.

Paul's unique experience as a psychiatric nurse, a prison governor, and a pastor give him insightful perspectives into the ways in which God reveals His glory supernaturally. This book is a road map into the heavenly realms, and a travel guide to the vistas of the high places in the Kingdom. *What on Earth Is Glory?* could revolutionize your life! I recommend this book to every believer.

Kris Vallotton
Senior Associate Leader
Bethel Church, Redding, California
Co-Founder, Bethel School of Supernatural Ministry
Author of *The Supernatural Ways of Royalty*

In recent years the glory of God has been reduced to sightings of gold, feathers, and other outward signs. Paul Manwaring is careful to enjoy the micro expressions of His presence and glory, yet dive deeper into what glory looks like on a macro scale. Paul's book expands the understanding of glory and how it will impact this next season of history. God's glory will not be confined to a sideshow at a conference, but will ultimately transform cities. For those who are seeking the "more, Lord," I believe Paul provides a map that may lead you to places where God's glory has not been expected. Read, follow, and become a vessel of His expansive glory!

Steve Witt
Senior Leader, Bethel Cleveland

CONTENTS

FOREWORD

THE Market for "self-help" books is large and growing. Even Christian bookstores are filled with such books. Some of them are good and useful, giving us Kingdom principles to help us to improve in specific areas of our lives. We all need to improve. But sometimes what we want is best obtained by pursuing something else. It's the fruit, not the goal. I believe that to be the case with the whole *self-discovery* process. We learn best about ourselves in the pursuit of Him. God-discovery is the best way to find yourself in a way that has eternal results.

Believers often miss the real benefit of the Good News and continue to live with poverty of soul. Such a place of deficiency need not exist in us—not if we discover how Jesus values us and what He actually accomplished on our behalf. Ignorance of that has caused many to live as prisoners, while being totally free. As a child, I heard my dad's story of when they moved chickens from one farm to another. They'd tie their feet and put them in the truck. Then they'd untie them upon arrival. Strangely, the chickens would still lie on the ground once they were freed. They thought their feet were still tied. Many believers mimic the chickens well—free, yet living as though bound.

People do well at recognizing the ache in the heart for more in life. This cry is often for identity and purpose. But the avenues taken to fill the void often make the cure worse than the disease. Some call a psychic on a tele-phone hotline or even dabble in dangerous thrills, hoping to find something to live for. Identity and purpose are missing from our culture in a big way. Pumping each other up to believe in ourselves is short-lived at best and usu-ally adds to the problem in the long run. It's really hard to stay psyched all the time. The need for true fathers has never been clearer. *Healthy* fathers bring that element of true identity to life. In a very real sense, we are a nation(s) of orphans. We must have spiritual fathers (and mothers) who know *the* Father. God-discovery is the beginning of real self-discovery.

God is raising up healthy fathers for this purpose: to help us all find our true identity as we discover the Father. These fathers have been changed by God and are secure in their role. This excites me to no end, for as a new Jesus People Movement begins, there will be fathers in place to help heal what has been miss-ing for so long. Thus, we'll be able to offer longevity to a movement. That is where Paul Manwaring and his wonderful book *What On Earth Is Glory?* come into play. Paul is a true spiritual father. He speaks to us as if we were his family gathered around the Christmas tree. Generously, he gives away the most won-derful gifts to each of his children: identity and purpose, all robed in unimagi-nable destiny. He can do this because he has discovered what the Father actually thinks of His children and has purposed for this planet. And it's good.

This just might be the most encouraging book you'll ever read. The fol-lowing pages are rich in Kingdom principles that anchor the reader into a biblical perspective on life. Sound familiar? I wish it were. It has largely been missing. *What on Earth is Glory?* is rich with insight and filled with exciting potential, all while liberating the heart to dream again. This book is an invi-tation to encounter the Father of life. You will no doubt find yourself in the process—but this time you'll actually like what you see. Come join the great adventure by saying yes to the journey of a lifetime.

Bill Johnson
Pastor, Bethel Church
Redding, California
Author, *When Heaven Invades Earth* and *Face to Face With God*

INTRODUCTION

W HAT *On Earth Is Glory?* may not be the book you would expect a
former psychiatric and general nurse, who has also managed prisons, to write. Further, anyone familiar with my ministry might reasonably
expect me to write about organizational government, personal discovery, or
strategic planning. But this book is about what lies behind and underneath
everything I do and teach. It is, if you like, an articulation of God's grand
idea—His strategic plan, vision, and mission.

Through my journey, beginning with my salvation at 15, I have had a big
picture of God and the world He created that has been slowly colored in. As
a nurse caring for those dying of cancer, I saw the work of God in man's ability to discover medical and surgical skills. I also learned, as I read Kathryn
Kuhlman after work in my small nurse's accommodation, that He still healed
without doctors. In my work as a psychiatric nurse, I came to learn that He
provided for the mentally ill in the same way. In my prison management
career, through many sociological discussions and the countless prisoners'
stories I encountered, this picture of human brokenness, God's compassion,
His power to restore us, and His way of including us as partners in the restoration process gained further clarity and detail. Now, as a minister, these
emerging truths and my desires for the solutions in the heart and Word of

God have come together with further study, observation, and training, and a picture of God's grand plan has become more apparent to me—the seamless plan of creation, redemption, and restoration.

At the center of this plan is the Person of Christ Jesus, in whose face, Paul says, we behold *"the knowledge of the glory of God"* (2 Cor. 4:6), the same knowledge that Habakkuk prophesied would fill the earth, *"as the waters cover the sea"* (Hab. 2:14). It is impossible, of course, to write a single book that can begin to capture even a few aspects of the knowledge of the glory of God seen in the face of Christ, and I certainly have not attempted this here. My goal has been to recruit any and all who are hungry to become students of this knowledge by providing a starting place for reading and holding together many of the biblical references to glory so that it takes on greater definition. The definition we give to glory will determine where we expect to encounter it. I believe a limited definition of glory has prevented many believers from recognizing the glory around them. An ecclesiastical definition, in particular, confines our expectations to glory in the Church, whether in the ancient traditions with their pomp and ceremony or in contemporary worship focused on experiencing the presence of God. But Isaiah says that the whole earth is filled with His glory (see Isa. 6:3). That statement demands a definition that creates an expectation to see and know the expression of God's glory everywhere.

I doubt there is a greater word than *glory,* except God Himself, for it holds together the entirety of the grand expression of His nature He is unfolding through time. As I have studied glory, I have found that divisions and categories I had previously held began to change as the inherent unity and interrelatedness of all that God is and does became more apparent to me. Ultimately, I expect that as the knowledge of the glory of God covers the earth, categories like "sacred" and "secular" will be erased and things like "natural" and "supernatural" will become less polarized in our thinking. Every aspect of our lives will take on the synergy that flows when our lives are reflecting and expressing the glory of God. As you will find in the coming pages, most chapters in this book set out to address a particular facet of glory, and what I hope you will see is that every facet is deeply connected and related with every other aspect. We cannot understand the parts apart from each other or apart from the whole. Glory demands that we learn how to hold them all together. Ultimately, I hope to recruit students of glory because, in this great plan of God, we are His glory carriers. Yes, Christ is the center of the plan, but in placing Christ at the center, God has placed us at the center, for He has placed us in Him and Him in us. As His Body, we corporately reflect His vast, unfathomable nature by individually contributing our own manifestation of His glory in every aspect of our lives and relationships. It is the glory of an awesome God. I often think of how His voice is like the sound of many waters and ponder that His ear must be able to hear every drop of water that flows over Niagara Falls. That ear, and the heart attached to it, can hear the cries of a victim and perpetrator of an offense at one and the same time. For us, such stretching of our thoughts and emotions at best challenges us and at worst causes us to polarize our views. But the more we study God's glory, the expression of His nature, the more we gain the capacity to allow its many facets to lead us ever deeper in comprehending and reflecting His magnificence, finally leading us into a life filled with wonder, joy, and worship—a life of glory.

As Sue and I sang at our wedding:

> *Lord my God, When I in awesome wonder,*
> *Consider all the worlds Thy Hands have made;*
> *I see the stars, I hear the rolling thunder,*
> *Thy power throughout the universe displayed.*
>
> *Then sings my soul, My Savior God, to Thee,*
> *How great Thou art, How great Thou art.*
> *Then sings my soul, My Savior God, to Thee,*
> *How great Thou art, How great Thou art!*
>
> *When through the woods, and forest glades I wander,*
> *And hear the birds sing sweetly in the trees.*

When I look down, from lofty mountain grandeur
And see the brook, and feel the gentle breeze.

Then sings my soul, My Savior God, to Thee,
How great Thou art, How great Thou art.
Then sings my soul, My Savior God, to Thee,
How great Thou art, How great Thou art!

And when I think, that God, His Son not sparing;
Sent Him to die, I scarce can take it in;
That on the Cross, my burden gladly bearing,
He bled and died to take away my sin.

Then sings my soul, My Savior God, to Thee,
How great Thou art, How great Thou art.
Then sings my soul, My Savior God, to Thee,
How great Thou art, How great Thou art!

When Christ shall come, with shout of acclamation,
And take me home, what joy shall fill my heart.
Then I shall bow, in humble adoration,
And then proclaim: "My God, how great Thou art!"

Then sings my soul, My Savior God, to Thee,
How great Thou art, How great Thou art.
Then sings my soul, My Savior God, to Thee,
How great Thou art, How great Thou art!

—Stuart K. Hine, 1949, 1953
(Inspired by Carl Boberg's poem, "O Store Gud," 1886)

Chapter 1

WHAT ON EARTH IS GLORY?

The whole earth is full of His glory (Isaiah 6:3).

WHAT Is the first thing that comes to mind when you hear the word *glory*? Perhaps it suggests images of gold and light, crowns and jewels. Maybe it calls to mind great achievements or heroic feats. For some, it speaks of what belongs solely to Heaven itself, a state of perfection and serenity far from the struggle and day-to-day experience of Earth, the state we hope to enter at the end of our earthly lives. For others it suggests what we have fallen short of because of sin (see Rom. 3:23).

Glory fills the pages of the Bible. But like many of the great, rich biblical words, I fear *glory* is often abstract and lacks immediate connection in our minds and experience. And the images it does conjure up—crowns or heroic deeds—don't seem to help us much in comprehending the significance of what Scripture means by the word. In his famous address, "The Weight of Glory," C. S. Lewis describes the poverty that many of us bring to an understanding of glory, a poverty that makes glory appear strange and confusing:

> There is no getting away from the fact that [glory] is very prominent in the New Testament and in early Christian writings… All this makes no immediate appeal to me at all, and in that respect I fancy I am a typical modern. Glory suggests two ideas to me, of which one seems wicked and the other ridiculous. Either glory means to me fame, or it means luminosity. As for the first, since to be famous means to be better known than other people, the desire for fame appears to me as a competitive passion and therefore of hell rather than heaven. As for the second, who wishes to become a kind of living electric light bulb?[1]

But Lewis goes on to explain that when he put aside his initial confusion, dug deeper into the language of the Scriptures, and allowed Scripture to challenge and expand his thinking, he discovered the reason Scripture resounds with the word *glory* and with promises that we will have it. He saw that glory is what we were made for (see Isa. 43:7).

This book represents my own journey into the language of the Bible in search of a deeper understanding and experience of glory. As it did with Lewis, the journey happened to me, but once it did, I found myself embroiled in a treasure hunt, in which a series of intriguing clues led me to one discovery after another. And eventually, I found that *glory* had begun to unfold in my mind and heart as the word that contained my deepest longings, my highest priorities, and my destiny—as well as the conviction that it contained those things for everyone else on the planet.

As a result of this unfolding, the promise of Habakkuk 2:14 took on an increasing weight and significance: *"For the earth will be filled with the knowledge of the glory of the Lord, as the waters cover the sea."* Interestingly, this verse is often misquoted by the simple omission of the word *knowledge*. This omission gives rise to a vision of the earth being gradually covered by a sort of vapor that drips down from Heaven and eventually engulfs the planet in bright gold. Wonderful though that vision might be, it can leave us waiting for an appearance of glory that is completely outside of us, distracting us from the powerful invitation in this verse—the invitation to *know* what glory is, and ultimately, to live in a world where everyone shares that knowledge.

Another reason we cannot afford to leave out *knowledge* from the promise of Habakkuk is that its omission turns the fullness of God's glory on the earth into a future event rather than a present reality. When the prophet Isaiah saw the Lord enthroned, he heard the angels declaring, "*The whole earth is full of His glory!*" (Isa. 6:3 NKJV). The truth is that God's glory is not far from us. It is actually the reality that surrounds us. The whole human history of "falling short of the glory of God" has not diminished it in any way. Neither has our failure to perceive it. It is impossible for us to erase God's glory from the universe. As C. S. Lewis wrote, "A man can no more diminish God's glory by refusing to worship him than a lunatic can put out the sun by scribbling the word 'darkness' on the walls of his cell."[2]

In light of Isaiah's vision that the earth is already full of God's glory, the prophecy of Habakkuk is God's promise that the gap between the immanent reality of His glory in the universe and our perception of that glory will be closed. The fullness of God's glory will be matched by the fullness of our knowledge. Understanding this promise, however, depends upon understanding what knowledge is. The Hebrew word translated *knowledge* in this verse is *yada*, the same word used in Genesis 4:1, which says that Adam "knew" Eve. *Yada* indicates an intimate, experiential knowing,[3] and what is more, one that results in reproduction. The very nature of *yada* tells us that the promise of Habakkuk will not be fulfilled all at once, but will unfold through a continuous process of relational encounters, just as Adam and Eve experienced in a lifelong covenant.

In our world of the Internet and modern viral marketing, we are increasingly aware of how quickly experiences can multiply, and I like to think that

WHAT ON EARTH IS GLORY?

these technologies are a parable of what this multiplication of knowledge may mean in part. Capturing an experience on a video or audio recording and sharing it with the world now takes hardly any time and effort at all. Through social networking Websites, one video clip can go overnight from one person to millions. One person can laugh at the antics of a little child, and with the sweep of a mouse, that experience can be transmitted to thousands of homes across the globe in seconds. The reproduction of information has become a part of our everyday lives.

Of course, *how* it will happen is secondary to *that* it will happen. We are promised not merely that we will know about glory, but that we will experience it, live in it, and encounter it. And because God's glory is a present reality, it is a promise that we are invited to experience now.

God's Expressions

I have found, as Lewis and countless others have through the centuries, that words are keys that can unlock experiences for us. A journey into the language of glory is vital in preparing us to perceive and experience the glory that fills the earth. Therefore, throughout this book, I will be exploring various words and what they yield for us in our perception of glory, beginning with the word *glory* itself.

God's glory is *the result of God expressing Himself.* In other words, everything He has made and does, and the attributes, nature, and power behind those actions, are His glory. It is said of artists that they do at least two things—they copy and express themselves. But God is the artist who has nothing to copy (at least to begin with), so He just expresses Himself. *"All things came into being through Him, and apart from Him nothing came into being that has come into being"* (John 1:3). He is the originator of all things. This reality positions us to look for the revelation of glory in the various ways God expresses Himself, and to have both glory and God's expressions expand in our field of perception. If we study God, we will become familiar with what glory looks like, and as we study His expressions, we will become more and more familiar with Him. What is God like? What does He say? What does He do? The answer to these questions will reveal His glory.

Our two greatest resources in studying the expressions of God are the Bible and creation—the Book of Scripture and the Book of Nature, as they have been called. Scripture identifies creation as God's expression, through which we learn who He is:

> *For since the creation of the world His invisible attributes, His eternal power and divine nature, have been clearly seen, being understood through what has been made...* (Romans 1:20).

When we look at creation, we see God. We see His invisible attributes in a mother's love for her children. We see His eternal power through telescopes that reveal an enormous universe full of unimaginably powerful heavenly bodies and events. Closer to home, we experience His power in great waterfalls, mighty oceans, and sunlight that travels 93 million miles and yet retains enough heat to warm this beautiful planet. We see His divine nature in the way He created the human body to heal itself. God expressed Himself in His creation, and He didn't hide it. He is *"clearly seen"* in what He made. How offensive it is that the study of creation has been so perverted by godless theories, when it was designed by God to reveal Himself to us! Society's refusal to acknowledge the Designer and Source of all that exists is a fatal rejection of the first principles for gaining the knowledge of the glory of God.

The Bible is also God's expression:

> *All Scripture is inspired by God and profitable for teaching, for reproof, for correction, for training in righteousness* (2 Timothy 3:16).

Though written by multiple authors in different languages spanning thousands of years, the Bible's consistent message and revelation of God is undeniable. As we read the Bible, God is revealed to us, and His nature, attributes, and power are written across every page. It is even more mind-blowing that this very text also invites us to be imitators of the awesome God it reveals! (See Ephesians 5:1.)

Creation and the Bible do not merely symbolize or communicate God's glory; they actually possess it in themselves. This suggests an expanded definition of glory, based on Romans 1:20: *Glory is the eternal value that someone or something has because it reveals, points to, and reflects the attributes, nature, and power of God.* This definition accords us glory, for we are among God's expressions that reveal, point to, and reflect His attributes, nature, and power. In fact, along with revealing God's glory, creation and the Bible not only reveal that we have glory; they also reveal that among all that God has made, among His manifold expressions, human beings were designed to relate to His glory in a unique way.

We will explore our unique relationship to glory, as well as the glory of creation and the Bible, throughout this book. For the moment, however, I want to draw your attention to the only other verse in Scripture in which we find the phrase "the knowledge of the glory of God." Significantly, it is referred to in the past tense, another confirmation that *yada* of God's glory is not reserved solely for the next life:

> *For God, who said, "Light shall shine out of darkness," is the One who has shone in our hearts to give the Light of the knowledge of the glory of God in the face of Christ* (2 Corinthians 4:6).

Here we find Paul comparing two creative acts of God. God's first creative act was to command light out of darkness. Later, He performed a similar creative act, one with equal power, drama, and impact. But this time, He commanded light to shine out of the darkness of our hearts.

What was the source of that darkness? It was a rejection of glory:

> *Because that, when they knew God, they glorified Him not as God, neither were thankful; but became vain in their*

imaginations, and their foolish heart was darkened (Romans 1:21 KJV).

In ignorance and deception, mankind turned from the light of God's glory, only to discover that there is no other source of light in the universe. That light went off when they turned from glory. But when the light went on again, it was a different expression. God, who had first expressed Himself as Creator, now expressed Himself as the merciful Redeemer. Thus, the "knowledge of His glory *in the face of Christ*" is different than the knowledge of His glory that Adam and Eve beheld in their innocence. In the face of Christ, we see the *eternal value* God has for us, evidenced by the price He paid to restore us to the place where we could behold His glory and be restored to the glory we had fallen short of.

The knowledge of the glory of God, the knowledge that Habakkuk prophesied would fill this earth, is revealed in the face of Christ. But according to Paul, the true significance of God shining on our hearts, the true effect and value of the knowledge of the glory of God, is this:

> *We all, with unveiled face, beholding as in a mirror the glory of the Lord, are being transformed into the same image from glory to glory, just as from the Lord, the Spirit* (2 Corinthians 3:18).

The knowledge of the glory of God, gained in this relational posture of beholding Christ, makes us like Him. In other words, the intimacy of *yada* does not merely reproduce encounters with Christ; it reproduces His nature and likeness within us.

We were first created and then redeemed in order to be like God. No other part of God's creation was designated to bear His image; and thus no other part of His creation has the same glory we have. As Bill Johnson regularly points out, "Yes, God does say that He won't share His glory with another. But we're not another." We are made in His image—glorious! We are His body, His Bride, and His children. We are not usurpers or pretenders; we are image bearers. The knowledge of the glory of God in the face of Christ reveals our own glory—the glory He made us to share with Him from the beginning. And if we were made for glory, then there is one question that must possess us: What on earth is glory?

Endnotes

1. C. S. Lewis, *The Weight of Glory & Other Addresses* (New York: Macmillan Publishers, 1980), 11.

2. C. S. Lewis, *The Problem of Pain* (London: HarperCollins, 1964), 41.

3. Blue Letter Bible, "Dictionary and Word Search for *yada`* (*Strong's 3045*)," Blue Letter Bible 1996-2011, http://www.blueletterbible.org/lang/lexicon/lexicon.cfm?Strongs=H3045&t=KJV; accessed January 31, 2011.

Chapter 2

THE GREAT REQUEST

Ask, and it will be given to you... (Matthew 7:7).

IT Is no mistake that Paul, the apostle most steeped in the Law of Moses, was the one New Testament writer who spoke directly of *"the knowledge of the glory of God"* (2 Cor. 4:6). For it was Paul's deep understanding of the nature and significance of the various *expressions* of God witnessed by Moses that provided his powerful reference point for understanding what he was witnessing in his own day—the knowledge of God's glory revealed *"in the face of Christ"*. In comparing what Moses knew to what his generation knew, Paul concluded:

> *Not that we are adequate in ourselves to consider anything as coming from ourselves, but our adequacy is from God, who also made us adequate as servants of a new covenant, not of the letter but of the Spirit; for the letter kills, but the Spirit gives life. But if the ministry of death, in letters engraved on stones, came with glory, so that the sons of Israel could not look intently at the face of Moses because of the glory of his face, fading as it was, how will the ministry of the Spirit fail to be even more with glory? For if the ministry of condemnation has glory, much more does the ministry of righteousness abound in glory. For indeed what had*

glory, in this case has no glory because of the glory that surpasses it (2 Corinthians 3:5-10).

You can almost see this "Pharisee of Pharisees" jumping out of his skin over the revelation that the glory of the Old Covenant, which he had spent his entire early life seeking to know, was literally nothing in comparison to the glory God had invited him to know in the face of Christ. I imagine that few of us today can appreciate the magnitude of this statement and what it must have been like to live in the midst of that history-making transition between the Old and the New Covenants. Paul gives us the place to start in our quest for a deeper knowledge of the glory of God. With the help of the Holy Spirit, let us see what we can learn of the glory of the Old Covenant, the glory Moses knew.

What Moses Saw

As familiar as the Exodus story may be, I suspect few of us realize that the many expressions of glory in it are the introductory themes in a symphony that crescendos *with us* knowing His glory in the face of Christ. But though Moses heard only those opening themes, he knew they were building up to something—something huge. Moses was the first person since Adam (except perhaps Enoch) to have a clue that God intended us to know (*yada*) Him. The fact that what he experienced had "no glory" in comparison to what God displayed in Christ is simply stunning to me because I have never met anyone who has seen as much as Moses saw, not by a long shot!

Let's take a basic inventory of the amazing God-expressions Moses witnessed. Imagine realizing as a young person that you had miraculously survived infancy in the midst of an infant genocide. Not only that, you had been saved by the daughter of the Pharaoh who had ordered that genocide and been raised in his palace. Moses apparently realized that he had been spared in order to do something to help his people, but tragically, his early efforts ended in murder and exile. Then, without warning, this destiny was restored to him 40 years later in the wilderness, where he saw a burning bush and heard the voice of the God of his ancestors: "I AM. That's My name. I am telling you more than I told Abraham, and Abraham was My friend. But I am telling you." After this brief introduction, God announced that He was sending Moses to deliver His people out of Egypt and bring them back to that very mountain. When Moses asked for a way to produce divine credentials for this mission, God equipped him with an arsenal of miraculous signs to put on display. He threw his shepherd's staff to the ground and it became a snake; when he picked up the snake, it became a staff again. (I need to say that I'd probably be good for the rest of my days on a burning bush, a rod, and a snake. Especially after picking up the snake!) He put his hand in his shirt and it became leprous; when he put it in again, it was healthy.

And all of that was merely introduction. The real excitement began when Moses courageously met with the new Pharaoh and initiated a supernatural "throw down" by demanding that Pharaoh discharge the entire workforce building Egypt. In the ensuing battle of the plagues, we can reasonably assume that Moses, having been raised in the center of Egyptian culture and religion, saw exactly how each plague systematically revealed I AM to be superior to every Egyptian god. More, as Moses released each of these devastating blows to his former homeland, Moses received increasing firsthand revelation of the Lord's favor toward His people and His judgment toward their enemies.

This favor and judgment culminated in the incredible drama of the Passover, which foreshadowed Christ's death in the Passover lamb and the blood on the doorposts. Though Moses did not have the full understanding of its significance, he probably saw to some degree how sacrifice, covering, and blood were essential elements of how God accomplishes salvation. The next day, he led over a million survivors of that dark night from the known to the unknown, from slavery to freedom. He saw the Red Sea part, crossed through it with the people, and watched the Egyptians drown when they tried to follow. In the wilderness, he saw miracles daily—manna and meat to eat, water out of rocks, and guidance and protection by the pillar of cloud by day and the pillar of fire by night.

Then Moses returned to the mountain with his people, as God had promised:

> Certainly I will be with you, and this shall be the sign to you that
> it is I who have sent you: when you have brought the people out of
> Egypt, you shall worship God at this mountain (Exodus 3:12).

But though everyone saw the cloud and the lightning and heard the thunder and the trumpet, only Moses got to go inside the cloud. He was the first to hear the Ten Commandments. He held in his hands the tablets hewn and written upon by the very finger of God. He was the first to receive the breathtaking vision of the Tabernacle. He was the first to know the nature of the covenant God wanted to make with His people. Let me remind you, the apostle Paul says that we have a greater glory than this!

To put this in context, remember that from the Fall up until that point there had never been a season in which God had revealed Himself so fully to human beings. In a few short months, everyone in Israel saw and heard more of God than anyone ever had! However, in comparison to Moses, they had barely seen or heard anything. He was the only one getting to experience everything firsthand. He was the only one God was speaking to *"face to face"* (Exod. 33:11).

But after *all* that, as if he hadn't seen enough, Moses asked God what I will always consider to be the most audacious request in the entire Bible: *"I pray You, show me Your glory!"* (Exod. 33:18). It was audacious because the person with the most of anything usually shouldn't need more. Moses knew that he had already seen the glory of the Lord in the cloud, and in every one of His expressions. Why wasn't that enough? But it was even more audacious, or better, *risky*, because of what Moses had learned through his previous encounters. He'd learned that God was to be feared—that He wasn't above reminding people that He could consume them in a moment (see

Exod. 33:5). He knew that as a murderer he fell short of the perfect Law God had entrusted to him. He knew that asking to see more of this perfect God could be the last thing he ever did.

But God didn't consume Moses, or deny his request. Apparently, God did not think Moses had seen enough, or that he had asked for something forbidden. He agreed to show Moses His glory!

Going Deeper

When I saw God's answer, I realized that I needed to go back and find a way to make better sense of Moses' audacious request. The first thing I remembered was that Moses had been making requests of God all along, from his first encounter at the burning bush. He'd asked to know the Lord's name, asked for signs, and asked God to send someone else to deliver His people. He'd inquired of the Lord at every step between leaving and returning to the mountain. He'd even been bold enough to ask God to repent from destroying the Israelites after they rebelled! And with every interaction, God strengthened a relationship in which Moses knew he could approach the Lord and expect an answer.

The next thing I saw was that in one of these many interactions with the Lord, Moses had received a specific word from the Lord:

> *Then Moses said to the Lord, "...You have said, 'I know you by name, and you have also found grace in My sight'"* (Exodus 33:12 NKJV).

Moses had received *grace* from the Lord. It's easy to miss this. Moses is generally not one we remember for his revelation of grace. In fact, the New Testament teaches us to associate Moses with the Law and *not* grace, as John wrote: *"For the law was given through Moses, but grace and truth came through Jesus Christ"* (John 1:17 NKJV). But the truth is, unless he had received grace, Moses the murderer would never have been able to approach God.

Probably no one knew that better than Moses, and he certainly made a point of reminding God of that grace throughout the conversation culminating in his great request.

Incidentally, in one of my favorite messages that I share with prisoners and ex-offenders, I stand in front of them with a 99-cent Bible purchased from the secondhand section of a bookstore. As I talk, I tear out the pages written by three writers who were either murderers or accomplices to murder. The first five books of the Bible are the first to go, followed by many of the psalms, and finally, all of the letters written by the apostle Paul. I am left with a greatly reduced Bible. Imagine having no Psalm 23, no account of creation, no "love chapter" in Corinthians, no Romans 8, not to mention the great stories of Abraham, Isaac, Jacob, Joseph, and the Exodus of the people of Israel.

I love to encourage these who feel so outcast that, just as it was with Moses, Paul, and David, so it is with them—the grace that redeems them also will give them the opportunity to influence the world through their changed lives. Without the contribution of offenders, the Bible wouldn't be the Bible. All of humanity has been blessed by the grace God gave to these men—grace given, in the cases of Moses and David, thousands of years before Christ paid the price for it. As helpful as it is to divide the Bible into Law and grace, Old and New, we must also remember these contrasting elements work together in telling a continuous story, from beginning to end, of *grace*.

So then, Moses knew that he could approach God by grace. But this doesn't fully explain the deeper motivation for his request. So I looked more closely at the events directly leading to Moses' conversation with God, and found that this request was born in tragedy. Israel had committed their first major sin before the Lord, a debacle that made their previous grumblings petty by comparison. Moses' triumphant moment to deliver the God-made stones of the covenant to Israel had become a shocking disaster. He had smashed them in a rage, perceiving that the covenant was already broken.

Thousands had died at the hands of the Levites, and the rest of them had been struck with a plague. But the final blow had been the worst: the Lord announced that He would not go with them to the Promised Land.

Separation from God is the worst consequence of sin. *"When the people heard these evil tidings, they mourned…"* (Exod. 33:4 KJV). Perhaps they felt in some way the grief that Adam and Eve felt when they had to leave The Garden. They were to be orphaned, cut off from their source of life and identity. Everything rested upon the conversation Moses had with the Lord on their behalf:

> *Then Moses said to the Lord, "See, You say to me, 'Bring up this people.' But You have not let me know whom You will send with me. Yet You have said, 'I know you by name, and you have also found grace in My sight.' Now therefore, I pray, if I have found grace in Your sight, show me now Your way, that I may know You and that I may find grace in Your sight. And consider that this nation is Your people."*
>
> *And He said, "My Presence will go with you, and I will give you rest."*
>
> *Then he said to Him, "If Your Presence does not go with us, do not bring us up from here. For how then will it be known that Your people and I have found grace in Your sight, except You go with us? So we shall be separate, Your people and I, from all the people who are upon the face of the earth."*
>
> *So the Lord said to Moses, "I will also do this thing that you have spoken; for you have found grace in My sight, and I know you by name."*

And he said, "Please, show me Your glory" (Exodus 33:12-18 NKJV).

Imagine a manager who has just found out that the owner of his company, after a catastrophic first quarter, is suddenly handing the whole thing off to him. That was Moses. Up to that point, he had mostly been taking orders and had only *just* glimpsed the policy manual and building plans. He knew this hand-off would doom the enterprise to certain failure, but he also knew that the Owner had every right and reason, after such a mess, to abandon it and move on to other things. Moses was humble and practical: "So Lord, You want me to lead Your people into the Promised Land without You. As You know, thus far I've been relying on You for what to do next. I have no idea what to do without You. I need to know Your way. I need to know the character and thinking behind what You do and say, and You need to remember Your love for this company, which is really Yours.

"Show me Your way, that I may know You." This request didn't necessarily strike me at first as audacious. But when I looked, it turned out that no one had ever asked God anything like this before. Moses had asked for *yada*. Not even Abraham, the man of faith, had asked to know God and His ways. This was uncharted territory in human-divine relations.

Once again, God's response tells us what to make of Moses' *first* audacious request. He said, "My presence will go with you." What does it mean? It means that God had agreed to show Moses His way, to grant him *yada*. *Yada* (experiential, relational knowledge) is God's way. God, rather than simply programming us with ready-made knowledge, releases it to us through partnership and relationship. But there can be no *yada*, no relationship, without ongoing, personal encounter. Giving Moses *yada* meant giving him His presence.

Of course, the presence was exactly what Moses desperately wanted—that was the sign of grace he was seeking for himself and for Israel. But notice, God never said that Israel had found grace in His sight. He promised to be with Israel only by promising to be with Moses. Here we see another aspect of God's way revealed to Moses. At the request of His friends—those who have found grace in His sight—God will extend grace to those who have not yet found it. And here we catch the opening theme that would crescendo in a thundering climax of grace extended to all of humanity through Christ, who lives in eternity to make intercession for us before His Father.

We can only try to imagine what it must have been like for Moses as the implications of God's response began to wash over him. In a few moments, Israel had been saved from abandonment and probable destruction. This was certainly cause for immense gratitude and relief. But the reason for this change was even more momentous. Moses had just been told that all this was being done on his behalf because he alone had been granted a place of unprecedented, unbelievable intimacy before the Lord. Years later, David affirmed this unique privilege when he wrote, "[The Lord] *made known His ways to Moses, His acts to the sons of Israel*" (Ps. 103:7). I believe this encounter, where Moses first asked to know God's ways, was where the door to this intimate knowledge first swung open for Moses.

It was there, standing before this door, that Moses made his *second* and most audacious request: *"Show me Your glory."* As I said in the previous chapter, glory is God's expression. It is God unveiling who He is by what He does and says. When God promised to go with Moses, God not only averted Israel's crisis, but He also gave Moses personal access to know what He was like. And Moses was not merely content to stand before the door of *yada*. He persisted in pushing it open further and "[coming] *boldly to the throne of grace*" (Heb. 4:16 NKJV). And this time, his request was personal. He was no longer interceding for Israel; he was a man before his God. "Express Yourself, God! Show me who You are! Show me Your glory!"

Yes, it was audacious. But it was the boldness of a man who understood that the opportunity of his lifetime had opened before him. And he wanted it more than anything in the world.

Our Invitation

In the next chapter, we will explore God's dramatic response to Moses' great request. There you will better see what Paul was talking about when he compared the glory Moses saw with the glory we are invited to see. Before we look at it, however, I want to appreciate the example that Moses gave us in asking to see God's glory.

When the "Toronto Blessing" spilled across the Atlantic Ocean in 1994, my wife and I began to visit churches where "God was showing up." Through this revival, which is still going on, many in the Body of Christ have learned to ask for "more"; it has almost become a catchword. We have heard many testimonies of great men and women of God who have made this great request throughout the centuries. But Moses is our true forerunner.

Moses took the lid off of the box before he built the box upon which God would sit. He asked of God in the Old Testament what many have been afraid to ask in the New. How many of us, even with the benefit of the cross, have been paralyzed by a deep fear which has us feeling unworthy of asking to experience (*yada*) more of God? This fear only remains because we have been cut off from the truth of the New Covenant. At the birth of the Old Covenant, only one man asked for *yada*, but in the New Covenant, Christ tells all of us to ask, seek, and knock, for our Father will gladly give Himself, His Spirit, to *any* who ask (see Luke 11:13).

The New Covenant is specifically designed to bring us into the fullness of the "way" God initially revealed to Moses—the way of *yada*. The grace that God is pouring out in revival is reminding us that He wants us to *know* Him—to encounter Him, to live in His presence, and to invite Him to express Himself through requests for more. Requests for more are not to be one-time events, nor something that we mature out of asking for, but a way of life. The posture of asking for more is, in my observation, a crucial element in continuing to flow with a move of God. We keep asking, and He keeps showing up. The outpouring of the Spirit is an expression of relationship.

Will you join Moses and boldly ask for more? *"Show me Your glory."* No matter what you've seen, whether great or little, there is more.

Chapter 3

GOODNESS AND GLORY

No one is good except God alone (Luke 18:19).

HAVE You ever noticed that Jesus had a distinctive way of answering questions? He often answered a question with another question, or with a story. Some of these responses appear so oblique at first that you wonder if they are really answers at all, and all of them usually raise more questions. But that was the idea. For one, Jesus was a master at discerning the motives of the mind and heart. His answers penetrated to the questions behind the questions and brought them to the surface. It is the skill of the master discipler, the same skill used today in life and executive coaching where the asking of powerful questions is the key to developing effective lives. For another, Jesus was a master teacher. He understood that the truth is something we only know by degrees. Each degree is not an arrival but a point of reference from which we can go on to understand new things. Thus His answers were designed to satisfy but also to make hungry. They were designed to make seekers and learners.

I think Moses' conversation with God in Exodus 33 shows us exactly where Jesus learned to answer questions—from His Father:

> *Then Moses said, "I pray You, show me Your glory!" And He said, "I Myself will make all My goodness pass before you"* (Exodus 33:18-19a).

At first glance, God's response to Moses' great request looks like a change of subject. Moses was asking about glory. God started talking about goodness. But He wasn't changing the subject. He was answering the question. In this simple response, God was already beginning to teach Moses about the nature of His glory. The first thing God wanted to *express* to Moses, the first thing He wanted him to know (*yada*), was that He is *good*.

I would love to know what Moses thought when he heard the Lord promise to make His goodness pass before him. When I first read it, it had that feeling of a curveball, a surprise. After a bit, I saw that God was answering the question. But then, I began to wonder if God was also answering another question behind the question. I wondered if the goodness of God was something Moses had been trying to understand. I wondered if perhaps this exchange was in parallel to the one that had come before it. When Moses asked for *yada*, the question behind it, the question the Lord directly answered, was whether Moses could still be God's man and lead God's people in God's way without God's presence. The answer was a definite *no*. In this second exchange, God's response to Moses' request for glory suggests that behind it, Moses was asking, "God, what are You really like?"

Throughout the centuries, men and women have struggled with the paradox that lies on the surface of the Old Testament account of God. They see a God whose acts appear to be in extreme opposition—showing great mercy, faithfulness, and deliverance one minute and showing anger and punishment in the next. It seems reasonable to imagine that Moses, who first lived and then wrote the first part of that account, might have been one of the first to wrestle with this paradox. In fact, perhaps the *way* he was seeking to know was the way of the One he had watched go to extraordinary lengths to set captives free, only to threaten to wipe them out and abandon them when they were disobedient.

This question behind Moses' request seems particularly likely, not only because God answered it by promising to let His goodness pass by, but because of what happened when He fulfilled that promise. The events on the mountain the next day presented Moses, and all those who read his testimony, with a resolution to the paradox of God's nature.

God gave Moses the following instructions in preparation for those events:

> *You cannot see My face, for no man can see Me and live!... Behold, there is a place by Me, and you shall stand there on the rock; and it will come about, while My glory is passing by, that I will put you in the cleft of the rock and cover you with My hand until I have passed by. Then I will take My hand away and you shall see My back, but My face shall not be seen...Cut out for yourself two stone tablets like the former ones, and I will write on the tablets the words that were on the former tablets which you shattered. So be ready by morning, and come up in the morning to Mount Sinai, and present yourself there to Me on the top of the mountain (Exodus 33:20; 34:2).*

This was to be Moses' third journey up the mountain, and we can discern the reason for it by comparing it with the previous two. Each time God had called Moses up the mountain, it was to prepare for and define the nature of the covenant He was going to make with Israel. The first journey, recorded in Exodus 19, appears to have been the shortest—God simply wanted to tell Moses to warn the Israelites not to come up to the mountain while the covenant was being made. After God declared the Ten Commandments and other laws and the people agreed to abide by them, God invited Moses up a second time for a 40-day meeting, during which He gave instructions for building the Tabernacle and carved the words of the covenant into the tablets of the testimony. Apparently after the first trip, Israel did not expect Moses to be gone so long; they began getting anxious that he was dead and went to Aaron for alternative leadership, which, as we know, ended in disaster.

When God called Moses up the mountain for a third time and told him to bring new tablets, He was indicating that He not only intended to show Moses His glory, but also that He was going to restore and renew that which had been ruined at the end of the last journey. Though He did not give His reasons for having Moses cut out the replacement tablets, it seems appropriate. Moses had to play a part in fixing what he had broken, as well as a larger part in the covenant-making process, now that he had been promoted in his role as mediator between the Lord and Israel. The Lord acknowledged this when, after declaring this renewed covenant, He said, *"Write down these words, for in accordance with these words I have made a covenant with you and with Israel"* (Exod. 34:27).

The first matter of business on this, the third trip, however, was the Lord's fulfillment of His promise in response to Moses' great request. To do this, He first hid Moses in the cleft of a rock and covered him with His hand. This tells us that while Moses had previously been in extremely close proximity to God in the cloud and the consuming fire, God was about to expose him to a new, far more powerful dynamic of His nature. God had called it His *goodness*:

> *The Lord descended in the cloud and stood there with him as he called upon the name of the Lord. Then the Lord passed by in front of him and proclaimed, "The Lord, the Lord God, compassionate and gracious, slow to anger, and abounding in lovingkindness and truth; who keeps lovingkindness for thousands, who forgives iniquity, transgression and sin; yet He will by no means leave the guilty unpunished, visiting the iniquity of fathers on the children and on the grandchildren to the third and fourth generations"* (Exodus 34:5-7).

Following this declaration, the Lord renewed His covenant with Israel and wrote the Ten Commandments with His own finger on the tablets Moses had brought. After this 40-day meeting with God, Moses returned, for the third time, to the people. Before, he had shown them the wrath of God. This time they saw something else:

> *It came about when Moses was coming down from Mount Sinai (and the two tablets of the testimony were in Moses' hand as he was coming down from the mountain), that Moses did not know that the skin of his face shone because of his speaking with Him* (Exodus 34:29).

Before I really studied this whole progression of events, I had a vague idea that Moses' face had shone because he had been in the fire, had been so close to God that he got a kind of supernatural sunburn. I hadn't really worked out the three separate trips and their differences, and I hadn't seen that Moses' face had shone after only one of these trips. I was reading this early one morning when I saw it all clearly for the first time. I saw that though Moses had been in the fire, it was not on this occasion that God showed him His glory—God had made a point of covering him. It wasn't the fire or the cloud that caused Moses' face to shine; that created the glory Paul spoke of in Second Corinthians. Certainly the proximity of God was a part of the equation, but the main difference on this occasion was *the declaration of the goodness of God*. Previously, 40 days and nights in God's presence had not had this effect; yet here, hidden behind the hand of God in the cleft of a rock, hearing of the goodness of God, Moses' face shone.

The Standard

This *goodness* was the glory Moses knew. This was the glory Paul compared with the glory we know in the face of Christ. The glory Moses knew and the glory we know do not differ in nature, however, but in fullness of revelation. The glory we know in the face of Christ is also the revelation of the goodness of God. It is simply the full revelation of that goodness. But we can only recognize fulfillment if we know the promise.

Let's take a closer look at this promise, the declaration God made revealing His goodness. He said:

> *The Lord, the Lord God, compassionate and gracious, slow to anger, and abounding in lovingkindness and truth; who keeps lovingkindness for thousands, who forgives iniquity, transgression and sin; yet He will by no means leave the guilty unpunished, visiting the iniquity of fathers on the children and on the grandchildren to the third and fourth generations* (Exodus 34:6-7).

Earlier I said that God resolved the paradox of His actions when He showed Moses His glory. The solution to this paradox is that all of His actions flow from the same source—His goodness. We see clearly in this declaration that God defines His compassion, forgiveness, and lovingkindness, as well as His punishment of the guilty, as expressions of His goodness. It is because He is good that He is gracious, slow to anger, and forgiving. It is because He is good that He does not leave the guilty unpunished. If you've read the Old Testament, you know that He expressed these two aspects of His goodness throughout the history of Israel. You could say that the goodness of God is actually the theme of the Old Testament. At every point in the story, He revealed His goodness.

Often we use the term *good* merely to express personal preference or liking. But when God calls something *good*, as He did when He created the world, He is saying that it is like Him, for He is good. His goodness is the standard that defines *all* good. Above all, as God revealed to Moses, His goodness defines a standard for our lives. Appropriately, God accompanied the declaration of His goodness by again carving the Ten Commandments into the tablets of the testimony. These were not rules imposing some kind of arbitrary, engineered order on the people; they were guidelines by which the people could understand the moral standard defined by the goodness of God. Without such guidelines, Israel wouldn't know what God meant when He used the terms *iniquity, transgression, sin,* and *guilt.* The Ten

Commandments revealed, in a preliminary measure, how we are to reflect the goodness of God, and in doing so, tell us that God wants us to reflect His glory, wants us to be like Him. This is the reference point for the glory Paul refers to in Romans 3:23. Without the commandments, we would not have the backdrop for understanding the righteousness we are invited and empowered to attain.

The Better Answer

This is how the first covenant came with glory—it revealed the goodness of God, His standard for life. However, in revealing this standard, it created what Paul called *"the ministry of death"* (2 Cor. 3:7). It is easy for us, because of the glory we know in the face of Christ, to look at the shining face of Moses and see in it the promise of humanity's redemption and restoration to God. But that is not what Israel saw. *"When Aaron and all the sons of Israel saw Moses, behold, the skin of his face shone, and they were afraid to come near him"* (Exod. 34:30).

Why were they afraid? Why was the revelation of goodness so frightening? For that matter, why had God told Moses that seeing His goodness would mean death? The answer is that God's standard, His goodness, like a sword, reveals the line between life and death. God revealed this first in The Garden when He warned that death would come of eating of the tree of the knowledge of good and evil. For sinners, the revelation of the goodness of God brings the death sentence. C.S. Lewis describes this well:

> This is the terrible fix we are in. If the universe is not governed by an absolute goodness, then all our efforts are in the long run hopeless. But if it is, then we are making ourselves enemies to that goodness every day, and are not in the least likely to do any better tomorrow, and so our case is hopeless again. We cannot do without it, and we cannot do

with it. God is the only comfort, He is also the supreme terror: the thing we most need and the thing we most want to hide from. He is our only possible ally, and we have made ourselves His enemies. Some people talk as if meeting the gaze of absolute goodness would be fun. They need to think again. They are still only playing with religion. Goodness is either the great safety or the great danger—according to the way you react to it. And we have reacted the wrong way.[1]

Thus, the revelation of the goodness of God solves the paradox of His nature. God is a holy God and will not compromise His standard. But His goodness also reveals our great predicament. It raises this question: If God both forgives sin and punishes the guilty, into which category do we fall, the forgiven or the guilty? Some people, perhaps, have thought they could live up to God's standard of goodness and fall into a third category, the righteous. But any who have seriously tried to be righteous have been quickly disillusioned. As Isaiah said, *"All of us like sheep have gone astray, each of us has turned to his own way"* (Isa. 53:6a).

The Ten Commandments, rather than revealing our great moral power, have revealed the truth that we are all guilty. This eliminates the third category and puts us all in the worst of the remaining two. And so the question becomes: How do we move from guilty to forgiven? The first answer God gave was repentance through animal sacrifice. This was the ministry of death, the endless bloodshed to cover endless sin. But eventually, a few people began to catch on to the idea that He might have another answer, a better answer. David, for example, realized that animal sacrifice only dealt with the consequences of sin, while sin actually begins in the heart. He saw that true alignment with God's standard of goodness required obedience and a clean heart, which only God could create.

David was a person who perceived the heart of God flowing from His goodness, as was, I believe, Moses before him. They saw that a good God, in revealing His standard for life, did not wish merely to expose our brokenness and inability to meet that standard, nor merely to make provisions for cleaning up the consequences of our sin. When David saw the brokenness within himself, he deduced that God's promise to show loving-kindness, forgiveness, and grace could only mean that He intended to do something to heal that brokenness, to create a clean heart and right spirit within him (see Ps. 51:10).

A few hundred years later, we find Jeremiah speaking of a new covenant, a covenant in which God would heal the brokenness of every person:

> *"Behold, days are coming," declares the Lord, "when I will make a new covenant with the house of Israel and with the house of Judah, not like the covenant which I made with their fathers in the day I took them by the hand to bring them out of the land of Egypt, My covenant which they broke, although I was a husband to them," declares the Lord. "But this is the covenant which I will make with the house of Israel after those days," declares the Lord, "I will put My law within them and on their heart I will write it; and I will be their God, and they shall be My people. They will not teach again, each man his neighbor and each man his brother, saying, 'Know the Lord,' for they will all know Me, from the least of them to the greatest of them," declares the Lord, "for I will forgive their iniquity, and their sin I will remember no more" (Jeremiah 31:31-34).*

This is God's promise that He would bring humanity into His goodness and bring His goodness into us. In this new covenant, this better answer, we would no longer be hopelessly shut outside of His standard; this is what is meant by the law being "in our hearts." And as you can see, the promised result of being made *like* God in having His standard within us is that we would *know* Him—"the least…to the greatest" will have *yada*. The door that opened to Moses at the moment of his great request is now open for us all.

I think Moses himself longed for this better covenant. When Joshua came and told him about other leaders who were prophesying to the people, he said, *"Are you jealous for my sake? Would that all the Lord's people were prophets, that the Lord would put His Spirit upon them!"* (Num. 11:29). Though Moses did not yet know of the fullness God would bring in the New Covenant, in which He would not only put His Spirit upon us but inside us, he knew that *yada* of God's goodness was not just for him but for everyone. But he had to wait for the necessary conditions—the conditions God named in the last sentence of His promise: permanent and full forgiveness of sin. And for the guilty to become the permanently forgiven, there had to be a permanent substitute.

When we say that the Gospel is Good News, we need to realize what that good really is. The Gospel is the full revelation, the consummation, of the goodness of God first revealed to Moses. In Christ, God not only declared His loving-kindness, compassion, and grace; He showed it in His supernatural ministry (the ministry He also gave to us) as He healed bodies and souls. In Christ, God forgave not some but *all* sin, transgression, and iniquity. In Christ, God fully punished the guilty, once and for all. And in Christ, through His resurrection, God brought us to life again, restoring us to relationship with Him, the source of life, and giving us a new heart and mind to know Him and reflect His likeness. On the mountain, God told Moses that no one could see His face, His goodness, and live. But in Christ, we live because we see the face of God and are being transformed increasingly into the likeness of His goodness, His glory (see 2 Cor. 3:18).

In the next chapter, we will explore the ministry of Christ on our behalf in more detail. But I'll close here by pointing out that Christ came, in part, as God's final answer to Moses' great request. It is true that God's plan to redeem us and bring us into the fullness of the knowledge of His glory (the promise of Habakkuk) was made before the world began. But because He is a relational God, the unfolding of that plan has depended at every point upon the cries, prayers, requests, and invitations of people. This request of one man to know the glory of God gave God His opportunity to respond with an answer that satisfied, but which also made seekers who followed, like David, ever hungrier to know the fullness of what He allowed Moses to glimpse from behind. And yet, God could turn His face to no man. So He finally answered Moses, David, and the rest by taking it upon Himself to make the great request on our behalf. He became a Man and asked God for glory. He hid us in the cleft of His body and in His dying, beheld the back of God. And after three days, God turned His face.

Endnote

1. C.S. Lewis, *Mere Christianity in The Complete C.S. Lewis Signature Classics* (New York: HarperCollins, 2007), 35.

Chapter 4

JESUS ASKS FOR GLORY

And now, O Father, glorify Me together with Yourself, with the glory which I had with You before the world was (John 17:5 NKJV).

ONE Of the first truths we learn as believers is that, *"All have sinned and fall short of the glory of God"* (Rom. 3:23). This is one of the first truths we learn as believers. We all begin the journey of faith by recognizing that our lives fail to live up to the standard that flows from God's goodness. Yet too many of us have neglected the promise hidden in this verse—the promise of what it means to be restored from sin. If sin is falling short of glory, then restoration from sin is necessarily restoration *to glory*. Restoration to glory is the true purpose of our redemption through Christ.

In fact, glory is the purpose for which we were created (see Isa. 43:7). From all eternity, God made us to behold and reflect His glory. Our falling short of that glory did not destroy that purpose, even though that fall brought death to us. It only meant that accomplishing that purpose would require restoration through resurrection. It meant that salvation would not merely be a matter of commuting a criminal sentence, but of taking the criminal and making him a man—the man he never was and yet was always meant to be.

When Moses asked his audacious question of the Lord, he was actually asking for something that God had intended from the beginning—from
before the beginning. In seeing past God's acts and coming to know His ways,
Moses also came to know His eternal purpose. Not only that, he himself,
by mediating grace to Israel and by releasing the revelation of God's glory
to them through a face-to-face relationship, became a *type* of the One who
would ultimately fulfill God's eternal purpose. Thus it was appropriate that
Moses was the first human to deliver a Messianic prophecy concerning the
One:

> *The Lord your God will raise up for you a Prophet like me from
> your midst, from your brethren. Him you shall hear...* (Deuter-
> onomy 18:15 NKJV).

That prophet about whom Moses spoke was Jesus, who in turn spoke
about Moses. After He was confronted by the Pharisees for healing a man
on the Sabbath, Jesus said to them:

> *How can you believe, when you receive glory from one another
> and you do not seek the glory that is from the one and only God?
> Do not think that I will accuse you before the Father; the one
> who accuses you is Moses, in whom you have set your hope. For
> if you believed Moses, you would believe Me, for he wrote about
> Me. But if you do not believe his writings, how will you believe
> My words?* (John 5:44-47)

Here Jesus gives us an outline of *faith*. He first says that faith means seeking glory from God. Wow. Then He says it means believing Moses. Finally,
as the consequence of believing Moses, it means believing Him. According
to Christ, our faith is to be directly involved with recognizing the relationship between Moses, who sought the glory of God and spoke of the Prophet
to come after him, and Christ, who came revealing the glory of God (see
John 2:11) and declaring the word of the Lord as that Prophet. Significantly,
John, who recorded this statement of Christ in his Gospel, also recorded the

testimony of one who had this faith—Philip, who said to Nathanael, *"We have found Him of whom Moses in the Law and also the Prophets wrote—Jesus of Nazareth, the son of Joseph"* (John 1:45). Philip believed Jesus because he believed Moses.

Jesus' description of how we believe resonates strongly with what Paul said about how we know the glory of God in the face of Christ; we know it in comparison to the glory Moses knew. Once again, the relationship between Moses and Christ is one of *promise* and *fulfillment*. We learn and understand their significance in relationship to one another. I remind you of this because the purpose of this chapter is to see how Jesus brought fullness (where Moses had only seen a promise) when He followed in Moses' footsteps and asked God for glory. Simply put, Moses' request brought the *revelation of* God's glory, but Jesus' request brought *restoration to* glory.

The Joy Set Before Jesus

Jesus' final prayer with His disciples before He went to the cross bears several similarities to the prayer in which Moses made his great request. As Moses had interceded for Israel, Jesus interceded for all believers. As Moses had asked for the presence to go with Israel, Jesus asked for believers to be with Him. And as had Moses, Jesus made a request concerning the glory of God. But where Moses had asked God to show him His glory, Jesus asked for far more. Let's look at a portion of His prayer:

> *Father, the hour has come; glorify Your Son, that the Son may glorify You, even as You gave Him authority over all flesh, that to all whom You have given Him, He may give eternal life...I glorified You on the earth, having accomplished the work which You have given Me to do. Now, Father, glorify Me together with Yourself, with the glory which I had with You before the world was* (John 17:1-2;4-5).

"*The hour has come.*" If you read the whole chapter, you'll notice that the Lord never brought up the fact that this "hour" was the hour of His death. He made no reference to the sacrifice He was about to make to pay for sin. His focus was entirely on the final purpose for and result of that sacrifice, on "*the joy set before Him*" for which He would "[endure] *the cross*" (Heb. 12:2). And that joy was His restoration to glory. Christ didn't ask to *see* God's glory, but to *be glorified* with God's glory—the glory He had with God before the world began. He asked to be restored to His eternal glory as the Son of God.

Here I find that we must expand our definition of glory. Jesus was not asking simply for God to express Himself. Neither was He asking the Father to reveal His goodness, or restore Him to His standard of goodness, for Jesus had always perfectly expressed that standard in all He did and said. The glory Jesus asked for was the substance and reality of God's very being expressed in the triune relationship that exists within Him.

As I said at the end of the last chapter, God became a Man so that He could make this great request of Himself—and answer it. And in answering it, in restoring His Son to His heavenly glory as a Man, He restored all of humanity with Him. He imparted the substance of His being to us and brought us into the mutual love of the Trinity. Thus, as we read on in Jesus' prayer, we see that the whole significance of "His" restoration to glory is that it was "our" restoration to glory:

> *The glory which You have given Me I have given to them, that they may be one, just as We are one; I in them and You in Me, that they may be perfected in unity, so that the world may know that You sent Me, and loved them, even as You have loved Me. Father, I desire that they also, whom You have given Me, be with Me where I am, so that they may see My glory which You have given Me, for You loved Me before the foundation of the world* (John 17:22-24).

Our restoration to glory was the joy set before Christ, for it accomplished two things that He and His Father had desired and planned in eternity. First, in giving us His glory, He made us *one* as He and His Father are one—He brought us into the relationship He shares with the Father. It is His glory that makes us sons and daughters, and this is exactly why the Father sent His Son, to "[bring] *many sons to glory*" (Heb. 2:10). This is also why He spoke of salvation, not only as a resurrection, but also as a *birth*. Babies do not simply come to life; they come into families. When the Father restored the Son to glory and made us share in His substance, He brought us into the family that exists in Himself between the Father, Son, and Holy Spirit. We need only remember Jesus' story of the Prodigal Son (see Luke 15) to see the great joy our Father has in restoring His sons to Himself.

Second, Jesus *desires* (the Greek word there is also translated "to love," or "take delight in"[1]) that, in this oneness created by giving us His glory, we will *be with* Him where He is. As I said, this is similar to Moses' request that God's presence would go with Israel. And yet it is different. For Moses' sake, the Lord promised that His presence would go with Israel, and provided them with visible signs that He was among them, culminating with His arrival in the form of a Man. But this Man did not only dwell among us. In His dying and resurrection, He brought us up to dwell in heavenly places with God Himself, and He sent His Spirit to dwell within us. So now God not only goes with us, but He also lives in us, and we live in Him.

The knowledge of God's glory in the face of Christ is something He has given to us, not by hiding us as He hid Moses but by bringing us into the deepest of relationships and closest of proximities. This has always been the great joy and desire of God—that we would be His, and be *with* Him. I hope you're beginning to see a bit more of what Paul saw when he said that what Moses knew had no glory in comparison to what we know.

Living From Eternity

In recent generations, it has been common to speak of being with Christ and being in glory as realities we will experience when we die. Certainly, there is the promise that in death, we will shed our "earthly tents" and be clothed in our heavenly "dwelling" (see 2 Cor. 5:1-2). Likewise, John says, *"Beloved, now we are children of God, and it has not appeared as yet what we will be"* (1 John 3:2a). There is absolutely a greater reality that we do not fully experience while we live in time and space. But Scripture also tells us that God *"has raised us up with Him, and seated us with Him in the heavenly places in Christ Jesus"* (Eph. 2:6). Likewise, Scripture says we *have been* made sons and *been* glorified:

> For those whom He foreknew, He also predestined to become conformed to the image of His Son, so that He would be the first-born among many brethren; and these whom He predestined, He also called; and these whom He called, He also justified; and these whom He justified, He also glorified (Romans 8:29-30).

The heavenly super-reality that we will fully experience in the future is also a present reality and a past reality—it is eternal reality.

As believers, we are called not just to look forward to this eternal reality, but also to learn to live *from* it, as Jesus did in His life and ministry. Paul put it this way:

> Therefore if you have been raised up with Christ, keep seeking the things above, where Christ is, seated at the right hand of God. Set your mind on the things above, not on the things that are on earth. For you have died and your life is hidden with Christ in God. When Christ, who is our life, is revealed, then you also will be revealed with Him in glory (Colossians 3:1-4).

Instead of thinking about what will happen when we *will* die, we are to think that we *already have* died. Instead of seeking to go to Heaven, we are to seek Heaven because that is where we *already are*. Our lives are to be a constant journey of learning what is eternally true about us and how to live from that reality on a daily basis.

I mention this here because of how it affects us as we attempt to do the first thing Jesus called an expression of *faith* in John 5. He said that believers "*seek the glory that is from the one and only God*" (John 5:44). We have already seen that Moses' audacious request was an invitation for us to ask for greater revelation of the glory of God, for *yada* encounters with His goodness. Yet in considering Jesus' great request and *what it did to us* eternally, we find that our seeking God's glory should be something even deeper than seeking encounters with Him. Moses, as a servant and friend, asked to see God's glory. Jesus, as a Son, asked to be glorified, and in His glorification, made us sons. Thus, He positioned us to make the same request. As sons and daughters of God, seeking His glory means joining in Jesus' prayer that we enter into the fullness of what it means to be *with* God and *one with* God. It means that, more than encountering our Father, we seek to live ever more fully in His presence, walking with Him as sons and increasingly displaying His nature in all that we are and do. As we say in revival circles, we don't want just to have visitations from God but to be the habitation of God.

Glory and Joy

I said that our glorification was the joy set before Christ. When we are still trying to wrap our minds around the idea that our salvation was not just about God forgiving our sin, it's difficult to imagine that both bringing us into His family and bringing us close to Him would bring God so much joy that He gladly endured the horror of the cross. But the more we know of His glory, the more we come to know why our sharing His glory brings Him joy. We come to see that the very substance of God is that He is a Father who delights in His children and created His children to delight in Him.

In creating us as His children for His glory, He created us for joy. Thus the Westminster Catechism superbly stated: "Man's chief end is to glorify God, and to enjoy him forever."[2]

It probably goes without saying, but delighting in one another as our Father desires requires being together. In one of his Messianic psalms, David sang:

> *I have set the Lord continually before me; because He is at my right hand, I will not be shaken. Therefore my heart is glad and my glory rejoices; my flesh also will dwell securely...You will make known to me the path of life; in Your presence is fullness of joy; in Your right hand there are pleasures forever* (Psalm 16:8-9,11).

When the Lord is before him and at his right hand, his *"glory rejoices."* The word translated "rejoice" also means "tremble." This makes me think of a tuning fork that vibrates when its note is sounded. When God is before us, when we are close to Him, we resonate with the same sound that is God. We rejoice in His presence, for in His *"presence is fullness of joy."* Our glory rejoices—the substance that we share with God is expressed in the intimacy and exchange of being *with Him* as Father and children, and that expression is joy.

In *Orthodoxy*, G.K. Chesterton said, "Man is more himself, man is more manlike, when joy is the fundamental thing in him, and grief the superficial."[3] And C.S. Lewis said, "Joy is the serious business of heaven."[4] God's purpose in restoring us as sons and daughters and bringing us close to Himself is nothing less than to bring us into joy. I submit that the level of joy in a person, a family, a city, a nation, and the world is the direct measure of how fully they have stepped into the knowledge and reality of the glory of God. Certainly, if His presence is fullness of joy, then our level of joy reveals the degree to which we have learned to live in His presence.

Jesus had much to say about joy in His final words to His disciples before He went to the cross. He instructed them to abide in His love and commands, explaining, "*These things I have spoken to you so that My joy may be in you, and that your joy may be made full*" (John 15:11). He promised that, though they would grieve for a time when He had gone, "*I will see you again, and your heart will rejoice, and no one will take your joy away from you*" (John 16:22). But then He laid out the great, heavenly blank check:

> *In that day you will not question Me about anything. Truly, truly, I say to you, if you ask the Father for anything in My name, He will give it to you. Until now you have asked for nothing in My name; ask and you will receive, so that your joy may be made full* (John 16:23-24).

Asking our Father for things in Christ's name is arguably *the* activity *par excellence* by which we walk in sonship. True sons and daughters ask their Father for things and receive them. And we can always identify whether our asking and receiving are genuine by looking at their fruit. When we truly enter into asking and receiving from our Father, the unmistakable result is *fullness of joy*.

After instructing His disciples to ask, Jesus showed them where to start asking in His High Priestly Prayer (see John 17). Some of us worry about whether we really know how to ask the Father for things in Jesus' name, whether we're praying in His will. But we simply can't go wrong if we ask for the same things for which Jesus asked, especially by asking for the thing that was uppermost in His mind and heart as He laid down His life for us. His greatest request and desire was that we be *"perfected in unity"* (John 17:23) with Him and each other through His glory. This request is to be the bedrock of our lives, for all of our asking and all of our living must flow from our constant pursuit to be one with Him and each other in every aspect of our being.

Jesus made it clear that this oneness would bring the world to faith:

I do not ask on behalf of these alone, but for those also who believe in Me through their word; that they may all be one; even as You, Father, are in Me and I in You, that they also may be in Us, so that the world may believe that You sent Me (John 17:20-21).

Here Jesus added to His outline of faith. Before He came, Moses and the Prophets were the key to recognizing Him for who He really is. But now that He has been glorified, He is to be recognized through His brothers and sisters. It is when our lives "tremble" with the extreme joy of living in the presence of our Father and walking as His sons and daughters that the world will recognize Christ as the One who came to restore them to the purpose for which they were created—glory.

Endnotes

1. Blue Letter Bible, "Dictionary and Word Search for *thelō* (*Strong's 2309*)," Blue Letter Bible 1996-2011, http://www.blueletterbible. org/lang/lexicon/lexicon.cfm?Strongs=G2309&t=KJV; accessed January 31, 2011.

2. James R. Boyd, *The Westminster Shorter Catechism* (Philadelphia: Presbyterian Board of Publication, 1854), 19, http://books.google. com/books?id=vyFMAAAAYAAJ&printsec=frontcover&dq=west minster+catechism&hl=en&ei=7tZETZsbi6KwA6LYhZMK&sa =X&oi=book_result&ct=result&resnum=1&ved=0CC4Q6AEwA A#v=onepage&q&f=false; accessed January 29, 2011.

3. G.K. Chesterton, *Orthodoxy* (New York: John Lane Company, 1908), 296.

4. C.S. Lewis, *Letters to Malcolm* (New York: Harcourt, Inc., 1964), 93.

Chapter 5

RESTORING THE HEARTS OF THE FATHERS TO THE CHILDREN

He will restore the hearts of the fathers to their children and the hearts of the children to their fathers, so that I will not come and smite the land with a curse (Malachi 4:6).

ONE Day, as I sat in a meeting listening to one of my favorite teachers, I began simultaneously having a conversation with God, sparked by a simple question that came to me regarding a new area of work in which I was embarking. "How do you father an organization?" I asked Him.

Now, this was not an entirely new question for me. I had begun asking it to some degree years before, during my previous career as a prison governor (warden) in the United Kingdom. In that capacity, I developed a thorough knowledge of senior management and discovered the efficacy of employing principles of fathering in leading prisoners. In fact, a book concerning the jailing of young offenders refers to me as someone who treats them as sons. (Sadly, on the other hand, I think my natural sons may have accused me at times of treating them like prisoners!) But when I began a career in ministry after 24 years of working first as a nurse and then in prison, I discovered that

I still had much to learn about leadership. (This is not to say that I, and many others, have not been or are not in full-time ministry working in prisons, schools, hospitals, restaurants, etc. I am so glad that the Kingdom culture of which I am part is recognizing that ministry by no means only happens behind a pulpit. After all, there is hardly anyone in the Bible who was in "full-time ministry"!) My ongoing desire to grow as a leader and a leader of leaders motivated this question.

As I had been initially surprised by His reply to Moses, I was surprised by God's reply to my question. He said that being a father requires first learning to be a son. And then, He got personal: "You stopped being a son when your father died."

I had been expecting a strategy, not a new inner healing journey. But God wanted to talk about my heart—wanted, as I discovered, to lead me into a deeper experience of the relationship with Him that Christ had brought me into by giving me His glory. When I reflected, I recognized the truth of what He had said, though it had never occurred to me before. On the day my father died, I stopped seeing myself with the identity of a son. I left sonship behind in 1973, at 15 years old. And the people around me—not only my family, my entire world—conspired, though with the very best intentions, to help with my rapid transition from son to independent man.

I remember hearing these encouraging words: "You're a man now. Help your mother. Look after the house. Make sure your mother's OK." My mother had a general store and post office in England at that time, so there was work to be done. There was a store to run, Cash and Carry trips two nights a week, and a house and garden to look after. I was reasonably competent and capable in life and could turn my hand to most things (apart from music and car mechanics—you don't want me to turn my hand to either of those). And so this self-reliant, fairly capable young man grew up, having stopped on that day—which, incidentally, was also the day I actually became a Christian—being a son. In this conversation with God, I realized that whenever I heard anyone talk of being a son, I visualized a 15-year-old boy at most. That's where being a son stopped for me.

I have since learned that this is by no means uncommon. Some people lose a father, some never know one, some have terrible experiences at the hands of a father, and others believe that they are to put their father out of a job by the time they are 18 or so. But as I pondered God's answer, I began to see that this was never meant to be.

The Pattern of Divine Relationships

As Jesus revealed in His High Priestly Prayer, our restoration to glory is by definition a restoration of relationship—in particular, restoration to being sons and daughters of the Father. From this position, we enter into the dance of divine relationship—into the family—that exists among the three persons of the Trinity. We are not only sons and daughters of the Father but also brothers and sisters of Christ. And like a mother, the Holy Spirit trains and raises us up in each of these relationships, ultimately making us into mature sons and daughters who will become the Bride of Christ for eternity.

But in bringing us back into this pattern of relationships in the Trinity, Christ has necessarily restored us to the divine pattern of relationships God designed us to have with one another. Genesis reveals that God originally created us in His image for multidimensional relationships—with Him and with each other:

> *Then God said, "Let Us make man in Our image, according to Our likeness…." God created man in His own image, in the image of God He created him; male and female He created them* (Genesis 1:26-27).

God is an "Us" who made humans to be an "us." His inherently relational triune nature is reflected, on a smaller scale, in those He made in His image, and thus it is only in relationship that we truly reflect His image. For this reason, theologians assert that the true "crown of creation" revealed in Genesis was not merely the making of man, but the making of a relationship—marriage—between the two individuals who, together, formed the image of God. Out of the bond of marriage are to come children, who then marry, who then have children, who then marry… In short, one way we were made to express the image of God is by having families ourselves.

In his letter to the Ephesians, Paul said that he bowed *before the Father, from whom every family in heaven and on earth derives its name*" (Eph. 3:14-15). The human family was named for God. Thus, it is undeniably glorious—it has an immense eternal value because it was explicitly made to reflect, point to, and represent the attributes, nature, and power of God. When families express a clean, clear reflection of the pattern of relationship in God, then they serve as highways or tutors that teach us how to participate in those relationships. And the more fully we enter into the relational life of the Trinity, the more we are able to reflect and perpetuate that pattern in our own families, from generation to generation. Human and divine relationships were made to be a beautiful tapestry that endlessly displays glory. This glory God gave to the human family is something that far too few of us have glimpsed, for the Fall rent the fabric of human and divine relationships. The highways that were meant to lead us to God and to one another have been terribly damaged, and from these gaps in our relational highways we have all inherited gaps in our grid for knowing how to handle what we experience. In my life, the highway of sonship was cut off at the age of 15, and consequently, my ability to relate to my heavenly Father was impaired. And because I had stopped learning to be a son, I hadn't received what I needed to know in being a father to sons. When my eldest son turned 15, I (perhaps unwisely) said to him, "I don't know what we do from here on because I haven't walked this part of relationship before." In relationships, as in everything, you can't give what you haven't received. You don't know what you don't know!

The unbelievably good news of the Gospel is that our restoration to glory in Christ has made a way for these relational gaps and losses to be restored. As I came to learn, the Father's revelation that I had stopped being a son was His invitation to experience this restoration. Significantly, He was not only promising to give me what I needed to learn to be His son; He was promising to show me how to be restored as the son of the father I had lost. He was showing me that I was never meant to have stopped being my father's son. Keeping that identity and relationship alive in my life was important because it aligned my human relationships with the pattern of heavenly relationships. Remaining the son of Douglas Manwaring prepares me to know my heavenly Father as His son through-out eternity, just as Jesus Christ remains the Son for all eternity—not only the Son of God, but also the Son of David. It also prepares me to know God in the dual role of son and father, a dual role we see expressed in the paradox of Isaiah 9:6:

> *For a child will be born to us, a son will be given to us; and the government will rest on His shoulders; and His name will be called Wonderful Counselor, Mighty God, Eternal Father, Prince of Peace.*

In eternity, Jesus, who had no natural earthly father or natural earthly sons, is the Son of God and Son of David, and He is also Eternal Father. Carrying the dual role as father and son not only prepares me to know God in eternity but also enables me to prepare my sons to step into that eternal pattern. In staying connected to my father, I am able to bring my sons into the chain of generational relationship. I think one of the most powerful pic-tures of this chain is seen in the last chapter of Job, where four generations of Job's family are alive at the same time. Job's son, for example, even being a grandfather and father at 110 years old, was still the son of his father.

Seeing these eternal relationships in God and how He meant them to be expressed throughout our lives turned my idea that it was normal to stop being a son on its head. Common as it may be, it is the exact opposite of what God has for us. Instead, He wants to rebuild our lives on the founda-tion of sonship.

My Healing Journey

And so I embarked on this new healing journey. I had stopped being a son, and at that point didn't know if I could begin again. So I began asking, "Is sonship something that I can get back? If so, how can I get it back?"

I first began to recognize what I had missed in not being a son by seeing what I had missed as a father. As I pondered the Lord's word to me, I recalled some things that my wife had said repeatedly to me over the years. She had often observed that my sons were at times more of a responsibility to me than a joy. As a result, I had left things for her to do that I saw as her responsibility. For example, she reminded me that when the boys were infants, I hadn't been willing to change diapers (*nappies*, to be exact—two nations divided by a common language and all of that), and so had missed some of the joy of being a dad. When she'd said this to me, it hadn't made any sense. For one, I thought I *had* done those kinds of things. But I had to admit that I had probably confused my memories of changing *other people's* kids' diapers during my 12 weeks in obstetrics while training as a nurse with what I had actually done for my own sons. When I began to understand what she had been telling me and that it was correct, I asked her forgiveness. It's painful, I know, but sometimes our wives tell us things about us that are actually true and that we need to change.

Some time later, I was going through our photo albums and scanning photographs for my wife to make an album for our son, who was getting married. I found and proudly scanned a photograph of me changing a diaper. Though I had asked for forgiveness, I thought I was right, and I felt vindicated—until my wife came home, saw the picture, and told me that the diaper didn't belong to either of my kids. It was my nephew's. So I again asked for her forgiveness and said, "You know, you were right." My wife is a good, patient woman.

From there I began to ask the Lord for more insight. He showed me even more clearly that when my boys were growing up, I had missed something. I love my boys, and anybody around me knows I love them. But I missed something. I missed it because when my boys were born, I saw fatherhood as yet another responsibility. The absence of my father at his grandsons' births robbed me of a celebration in which a father sees his son become a father while remaining his son. That adding of generations is meant to be one of those experiences that lead us into our eternal identity and bring us more fully into the great joy of being part of God's family. But with no father to celebrate my fatherhood with me, I simply became a man who had another responsibility and did what men often do in that situation—I worked harder and longer, which further compounded the problem. (I think that letting kids become just another responsibility is actually one of those potential "man weaknesses," like the inability to ask for help and directions.) While our life was good in many respects, I had taken it a little too seriously and overemphasized fulfilling what I believed were my responsibilities.

When I saw this, I repented to God and asked for forgiveness. I said, "I am sorry that I stopped being a son. You intended me to be a son for all my days on this earth, and for all of my time in eternity. It is a part of my identity that I will forever have, but I left it behind at 15 years old." I compared this to having a "gap" in my highway of relationships, but you could also liken it to an artery that is meant to be filled with blood flowing from a father to a son, and to the son's son, on through the generations. We are meant to go on learning life through the eyes of a son, even when we become fathers, grandfathers, or even great-grandfathers. But in my case, there was no blood flowing. There was a blood clot—spiritual atherosclerosis, as it were, that had cut off the flow of life from my father for over 30 years.

After I repented, I decided to try using a tool that I learned from Pastor Bill Johnson. He explains that because we have been given the mind of Christ, we should not fear the imagination, as many Christians seem to, but instead should learn to use a "sanctified imagination" in the process of renewing our minds. (We had just better know when it is turned on.) I decided that I would use my sanctified imagination to invite my father into my life and reconnect with him. I would introduce him to the years from 15 to 47. I would introduce him to my wife and my sons, to the work that I had done, to my triumphs and my disasters. And I decided that I would never stop being his son. I was still his son, even though he had gone home early.

I am aware of the concern that using our imaginations in such a way could lead us astray into deceptions, like the guided imagery of the New Age, but I firmly believe that the New Age has merely perverted an ability God gave us for our good. My criteria for these experiences are that the Holy Spirit must be our tour guide, they must be congruent with Scripture, and the outcome must draw us closer to Jesus! I can certainly say that using my imagination to reorient my perceptions and self-understanding did just that.

Up until that time, I had always focused on what I lost. Some of you might relate to this mindset. I am pretty good at mental arithmetic—I can calculate very quickly (likely due to the training in my mother's store). Before this encounter, whenever anyone older than 51 died (the age of my father when he died), I would work out how old I would have been if my father had reached the age of that person. It was a mindset, a way of working out what I had lost. I actually had dealt with this habit before this but had never really gotten to the bottom of where it came from. Now I saw that this focus on what I lost had kept me from seeing what I had and had kept me from being a son. It was constantly leading me to notice, "Oh, I didn't have that experience. My father wasn't there when I got married, had kids, etc."

In this imaginative journey, I reversed that focus by bringing my father into my life, into what I had. I "introduced him" to my boys, told him the things they loved, the things they did that were like him, and the things they were passionate about, like music and soccer. I told him about my career and the things he would have loved. I knew I wasn't talking to a ghost. In Matthew 22:32, Jesus makes a point that the dead in God are truly alive: *"'I am the God of Abraham, and the God of Isaac, and the God of Jacob'? He is not the God of the dead but of the living."* My dad's in Heaven and if the Lord has willed it, likely knows these things already. It's even more likely that in the presence of the heavenly Father, he has a much fuller understanding of my life and our family than I do. But God was putting me back in context, reconnecting my heart to the man, Douglas Manwaring. In those moments, I became a son to him again after 32 years.

Through this experience, I *redeemed* those years that I had lost. I opened the spiritual artery so that life could flow from my father to me through each of those years, and in doing so, those years took on a positive value and purpose. We often see only a single dimension of redemption, the part where you take an empty soda bottle and get the money back, or redeem a gift certificate or coupon for a discount. But there is another dimension to redemption, which is really the more important. You don't just take the soda bottle and get the money back. The bigger thing is that the bottle can be used again. "Redeem" really means that you recognize the value of something and bring it back to a place where it can be used for its original purpose. There was much in those 32 years that was meant to benefit me as a son, but I hadn't received it as long as I wasn't walking in that identity. In becoming a son to my father again through my imagination, I was inviting God the Father to redeem the value and purpose of those years and restore their benefits to me. It might seem a little weird, but it was something I felt the Lord told me to do, and it changed my mindset from that day to this.

Restored

After I had repented and redeemed, I began to get restored. (I don't often use alliteration, but it works here.) I began to experience life as a son again. To "restore," for me, means filling up the pantry again. My "son pantry," so to speak, had been empty. Actually, I didn't really have one. I didn't have this place that I could go to as a son and get the things that I needed for life, the things that I needed in order to relate to other fathers or to my heavenly Father, and beyond that, to every relationship in my life.

God began to reveal things to me that restored my son pantry. First, He gave me a picture. He said, "Imagine yourself sitting around the family table. Times are tough, but you've just received some extra money. What would you do? The only thing you know it's OK to do is to be responsible and pay the bills." He showed me that I believed I could only have joy when every-thing around the table was OK. I never had a father who walked into that scenario and said, "Yep, I know times are tight, but let's just have a treat. Let's go out and have some fun." That's a picture of God the Father and the way that He wants to relate to us, but it was a picture I didn't have! I had to have everything be OK before I could say that my life was good and full of joy. And the truth was that "OK" never came. I saw that as long as I was waiting for the circumstances to be perfect, I would never enter into the joy the Lord had for me. He wanted me to see that I could have joy when things weren't OK; in fact, it's that joy in tough times when the joy of the Lord truly is our strength.

I also had a problem asking for help because I hadn't walked through those years of becoming an adult when you are learning and you can ask your father for help. God showed me that exposing your need is not a weak-ness. It's actually the opposite—it's a strength! We need look no further than Jesus, who constantly asked His Father for what He needed. Not being a son prevented me from learning that, so even though it might seem strange, it just never was my first port of call to ask God or anyone else for help. I was an independent, capable man who took my responsibilities seriously.

In the same week that I got the revelation about asking for help, some-thing else happened to me. A spiritual father gave me an extravagant gift that I didn't need. I realized when he gave it to me that it was the first such gift I had received from a father in 32 years. And then I realized that God the Father gives like that too. I hadn't been able to let Him give to me like that, though, because I hadn't expected it. I hadn't had the adult experience of a father who gave me what I didn't need, gave to me extravagantly, gave to me because he wanted to bless me, gave to me because he loved me. I had given my sons extravagant presents over the years, so the giving part was familiar to me. But the receiving part was new.

Next, I started to realize that I'd had almost a phobia of adult male-to-male affection. This was certainly appropriate while working in prison for 19 years; as you know, prison is not really an appropriate place to show male-to-male affection! But that was no longer true in my new career. I started to find fathers who would show me affection, and I learned to show them affection. I also started to show affection much more deliberately to my two sons. I kissed my son James at the airport when he returned from across the Atlantic. I'm not sure that I had ever experienced that dimension of relationship, even before my father got sick.

All of these revelations and experiences "restored" my pantry. When relating to God, I was able to start thinking, *Wow, I have a God who wants to give me things I don't need. He just loves me, and He wants me to enjoy life. I have a God who will walk into tough situations and bring joy. I don't have to have solved everything around me to put a smile on my face, have joy in my spirit, and say, "God is good."* This spilled over into my other relationships, and I began to find myself able to engage, connect with, and relate as a son to fathers in my life. I also began to recall moments when my father and grandfather had spoken into my life. Now that I was a son again, recalling these words became valuable, empowering memories. Not only had the value of the lost years been restored; the value of the years I'd had with them had increased.

The Last Word

The last word of the Old Testament is the prophecy of Malachi 4:6: "*He* [the prophet Elijah] *will restore the hearts of the fathers to their children and the hearts of the children to their fathers, so that I will not come and smite the land with a curse.*" God is intensely interested in restoring the generational bonds that enable life to flow to His people, and through us, to all of creation.

When the Lord told me that I had stopped being a son, it was because He had already begun the process of fulfilling Malachi's prophecy in my life. One important event in that process had already happened—I had received prayer from Leif Hetland, one of my favorite preachers. Leif prayed a simple prayer that God would enlarge my heart. That prayer changed my life. Leif prayed for me in September. After Christmas that same year, I said good-bye to my son James at the San Francisco airport. Farewells are hard, but this one hurt more than any other up until then. It was not by any means our first time saying good-bye since we came to live in America, but it was the hardest to that point. For days after, I felt the pain of separation from my son. My heart had been enlarged. I cannot explain it except to say that my capacity to love and be loved had increased. The heart of this father had been turned closer to the heart of his child, and this prepared me to turn my heart as a son to my own father.

No matter how broken or even nonexistent your natural family is, God has made full provision for you to be restored in your identity, first as a son or daughter, and then as a mother or father (even if you don't have natural children!). Your stories will obviously be different than mine in terms of what needs to be restored and how that restoration happens. But I can tell you with absolute certainty that it will happen, if you receive what Christ did in making you a son or daughter of God and allow His Spirit of adoption to lead you in accessing and experiencing all the benefits of that relationship. And with these benefits, you will be able to create a new legacy of glory in your family that will bless generations to come.

Chapter 6

GLORIOUS SONS AND DAUGHTERS

The Spirit Himself testifies with our spirit that we are children of God, and if children, heirs also, heirs of God and fellow heirs with Christ... (Romans 8:16-17).

WHEN I was trained in the prison service, one of the things we were taught to be aware of was something called role stripping. When a man goes to prison, he is stripped of his name, his identity, his clothes, and his personal possessions. He is then given a number and a prison uniform and put in a cell. This has a powerful effect on how he sees himself. I've always been a pastor in my heart, so when I worked in prison, I saw my job as caring for people. I understood how hard and frustrating it would be to be role stripped, to no longer be the breadwinner, or the father, or the son, or the husband—to be robbed of identity. But now that I am a pastor, I have come to see that role stripping is far more widespread. In fact, all of us to some degree suffer the consequences of having been stripped of our generational identity. This is what the curse has done to us. The reason the hearts of the fathers and sons have turned away from one another is that these identities were stripped from us in the prison of sin.

Fatherlessness is a curse—and as the term implies, it is a curse that works in the negative, through inactivity and lack. Fathers are a vital key for imparting identity to their children. Without fathers, it is more difficult for children to discover who they are. They are left to work their way through life independently, without the capacity to access the incredible benefits planned for them in the design of families. And because they cannot give what they never received, the fatherless may reproduce children, but they will also reproduce fatherlessness in those children. The curse is that the earth has been populated with people who live without the identity of being a son or daughter.

But Christ has fulfilled the prophecy of Malachi 4:6. First, Scripture tells us that Christ became a curse for us (see Gal. 3:13). At the cross, He took on the curse of our fatherlessness when His own Father turned His back on Him. Then, He fulfilled the role of Elijah, who represents a father, one who passes a mantle from father to son. Christ was the "Everlasting Father" who restored us to the Fatherhood of God by passing His mantle of sonship to us. And in doing so, He turned the hearts of the fathers to the sons, and the sons to the fathers. He restored the roles and identity that had been stripped from us and showed us a way out of the hopeless cycles of destruction that inevitably result from living without those roles and identity. He reversed the inactivity and lack of fathering by bringing us into the active love and provision of our Father. In passing the mantle of adoption to us, Christ has called us to extend that mantle of adoption to our own families and those around us, and it is more crucial than ever that we do so. Today, we are surrounded by millions of fatherless kids due to promiscuity, divorce, and death. In the vacuum of "father love," homosexuality increases as men turn to one another for this affection. This only reinforces the vacuum of male-to-male affection in those who aren't homosexual because they are afraid to appear so.

The list of problems that fatherlessness causes is long and frightful, and we must begin to show people how to reverse the curse in their lives by receiving the identity and affection that Christ has for them. But we must also be aware that we have an enemy who is very interested in keeping people under the curse of fatherlessness. First, he wants to keep us from reconnecting with Father God because he knows that, as Jesus prayed in John 17, our oneness with God will bring the world to faith. Second, he specifically targets our family relationships because he knows that if the hearts of the generations turn to each other, they will not only reverse the curse, but they will also release a blessing in the land that will put him out of business.

Christ Is the Model Son

Some time before the Lord showed me that I had stopped being a son, I had asked Him another question in another meeting. Kris Vallotton was preaching on the response Peter gave to Jesus when He asked, *"Who do you say that I am?"* (Matt. 16:15). Kris made this statement: "Who Jesus is *to* you is who He will be *through* you." That statement prompted me to ask: "Who are You to me, Jesus?"

Later, as I was reading the Bible one day, I realized that Jesus was a Son. So I began to pray, "I want to be a son. I want You to be a son through me, Jesus." I am not sure I knew what I was asking at that point, but given the events I described in the last chapter, I believe my request has begun to be answered. And I know the rest of my life will be a journey of accessing and manifesting that truth.

As I said before, we only give what we have received. Extending the blessings of adoption begins with learning to walk in our role and identity as sons and daughters. And this essentially comes down to learning to imitate Christ. The life of Jesus, from prophecy to birth, baptism, and ministry, models a path for us to follow in order to reconnect the generations and allow the blessings of fatherhood to flow.

Some years ago I read that in the culture of Isaiah's day, there was a practice in which the male child of a rich nobleman would be given to a senior servant in the house. His task was to raise the child, and when the child reached the age of responsibility, the child was presented to the father as a son. At that point the father would declare, "This is my son, in whom I am well pleased." The implication was that the son was authorized to represent his father fully in public life and business. It was the father's promise that if the son did something in his father's name, his father would back it up. In Jesus' case, His father Joseph was the "senior servant" who raised him to the age of responsibility, and His baptism by John was the occasion in which God the Father declared, for all to hear, *"This is My beloved Son, in whom I am well-pleased"* (Matt. 3:17). In other words, God promised: "Whatever My Son says, I will back Him up." The supernatural fruit of Jesus' ministry is a testimony to His faithfulness to His Father's business. His Father backed His Son up every time, for everything He did was in His name.

We have much to learn in our Western culture about establishing children in their identities as sons and daughters and then giving them this kind of affirmation, promotion, and commission as they make the passage to being fathers and mothers. This is an important piece in aligning our human relationships with the pattern of relationship in God. For we, incredibly, are called as Christ was to mature as sons and daughters who can learn to be about our Father's business with the same confidence Jesus had, the confidence that our Father will back us up when we do what He is doing and say what He is saying. When we do the works of Christ, we are writing checks in our Father's name, and we can trust that He will pay them out of His royal treasury. But we all need to hear our Father's voice declaring who we are, expressing His delight in us, and promising to back us up as we represent Him.

Qualities of Sonship

We will grow in our capacity to enjoy and carry glory by embracing the qualities of a son or daughter of God. So let's allow the Son of God to train us to walk in sonship as He does by briefly highlighting a few key qualities, which follow.

Sons and daughters have the ability to ask. As I have mentioned, asking is probably the primary expression of sonship, and as I described in the previous chapter, it has been one of the main things I have been learning to do as I am being restored as a son. Jesus gives me, and all of us, the perfect example. He told us to ask—He said it at least six times in His final conversation with His disciples before the cross. He explained why we should ask, and why we can trust the Father to answer. And He modeled it throughout His ministry, especially in His powerful High Priestly Prayer.

The character of a son is revealed in his ability to ask a father, trusting that the father will not reply out of control but love. Asking is an act of faith that believes and wants the best. Asking requires us to master our fear that we won't get what we want or may hear something we don't want to hear. Only when we push past this fear can we experience and trust the heart and blessing of a good father.

Sons and daughters are secure in identity. Secure identity flows from a father who is secure in his identity. I love how Bill Johnson describes the way he used to cheer his sons on when they were playing baseball! Whenever Eric threw a strike, Bill would shout from the bleachers, "Whose son is that?" Occasionally today he will do the same thing in church when one of his sons or his daughter is rocking the house with worship or revelation. The point is simple yet profound. In this simple cheer is the deep awareness that his son's or daughter's achievements are not a threat to him, but are, in fact, the complete opposite. They make him look greater. Even Saul, on observing the great victory of the newest member of his army, knew this truth and inquired, *"...whose son is this young man?"* (1 Sam. 17:55).

It is exactly the same with the Father and Jesus. The Father sent His Son to fulfill a set of assignments for Him and everything that Jesus did, rather than threatening God's position, enabled man to actually see how amazing God is. In fact, Jesus explained that the awesomeness He demonstrated as the Son was exactly what *glorified* the Father. The same is true of us. Living on this planet as sons and daughters, we have been given the opportunity by our lives and achievements to make God known and make Him look great! Our Father's security in us makes us secure in Him, and this frees us to be all that we can be. Imagine *God* shouting from Heaven over you—*"Whose son is that?!"*

Sons and daughters serve the King and the people. I love the imagery and language used in the church culture I belong to encouraging us to see ourselves as princes and princesses. After all, we are sons and daughters of the King! (Kris Vallotton has covered this subject brilliantly in his books.)

The role of a true prince or princess is to serve the king and the people, a role that I believe the late Princess Diana carried out to the highest level. Perhaps it only really became clear how well she had done this after she died, when she was hailed as "the people's princess." This title may have been given in response to a perceived lack of recognition by the royal family, but whatever the mixture of motives, it was true. She had made friends with the dying and hurting of the world, visiting hospitals under cover of darkness, knowing that her presence in the room of a child suffering from an incurable illness would bring hope, joy, and comfort to the child and his or her family. She knew what she carried. She carried a glory, which was in part representing the royal family, and we must also carry the glory that represents our royal family. We should walk through life aware of our mandate to bring hope, joy, and comfort to a hurting world, confident that when we show up, we make a difference!

The son of a king will serve the king and the king's subjects. Jesus came to do this: *"For even the Son of Man did not come to be served, but to serve, and to give His life a ransom for many"* (Mark 10:45). And like Christ, we are sure to have amazing benefits that enable us to fulfill the service to which we have been called. We must be confident that God has provided every resource we need to do what He has asked of us. A royal family is certain of their inheritance. Except in unusual circumstances, they do not typically live wondering if the palace will go into foreclosure or the family will declare bankruptcy. They live knowing that they will *"inherit a blessing"* (1 Pet. 3:9)!

This ability to be royal representatives secure in our identity gives us the confidence to run with our assignment, even when that assignment is literally out of this world. The incredible assignment of the king's sons and daughters is to bring all of creation into *"the freedom of the glory of the children of God"* (Rom. 8:21). This assignment begins by receiving the spirit of adoption and stepping into our new identity—*"the revealing of the sons of God"* (Rom. 8:19)—sons and daughters, who are predestined, called, justified, and glorified (see Rom. 8:30). We are the glorious sons and daughters of the King, authorized to restore creation to the glory our Dad gave it when He made it!

Chapter 7

THE GLORY OF RELATIONSHIPS

He who finds a wife finds a good thing and obtains favor from the Lord (Proverbs 18:22).

IN 2006, my eldest son, James, married his bride, Amy, after a six-year courtship and engagement. My wife, my youngest son, Luke, and I traveled to the wedding in England. It was a grand and emotional wedding, but no one had prepared me for what I experienced. As a father of two sons, I had often heard people say, "At least you don't have a daughter." Then they would tell me how emotional the walk down the aisle was for the father of the bride. I love my sons, but these comments had made me feel that I might miss out on something. I never had a discussion with anyone else about being the father of the groom, so I didn't know what to expect.

It was wonderful, but I was emotionally drained the day after the wedding. As I sat eating Sunday lunch, I asked God why I felt like I did. His reply opened a door into His heart, which completely changed how I felt from that day on. Quite simply, He told me that as I watched my son, who had walked in purity waiting for his bride for six years, I had caught a glimpse of His heart and how God, the Father of the Groom, is waiting for His Son to get His Bride! This thought was completely new, but it made perfect sense. The consequence of this truth, which we know but don't often express, is that for all eternity we will be the daughter-in-law of God! That describes one aspect of how we become joint-heirs with Jesus. We fall in love, take the family name, and like daughters-in-law, become joint-heirs with the Son.

More than any other New Testament writer, the apostle John used bridal imagery in describing our relationship with Christ, particularly in his Gospel and in the Book of Revelation. It begins when he quotes John the Baptist: *"He who has the bride is the bridegroom; but the friend of the bridegroom, who stands and hears him, rejoices greatly because of the bridegroom's voice…"* (John 3:29). The New International Version says the friend *"waits and listens for"* the bridegroom.

Why does the "friend of the bridegroom" wait for the bridegroom's voice? At that time in Jewish culture, the tradition was that the engagement was the most important event—the decision you couldn't retract from. You couldn't decide to take the ring back to Zales and get your money back because, once you were engaged, you were engaged. That was it. Following that event, the bridegroom went back to his father's house to prepare the place for them to live. The bridegroom left his good friend, the best man, with the bride to make sure that she was kept pure and to help her get ready for marriage. That is why he was the *best* man! He was the one whom the groom could trust with his most valuable relationship, his bride-to-be. And when he heard the bridegroom's voice again, he knew it was time to deliver the bride to him.

The picture is beautiful, and helps us to understand the language of the Gospels. Jesus said:

> *In My Father's house are many dwelling places; if it were not so,*
> *I would have told you; for I go to prepare a place for you. If I go*
> *and prepare a place for you, I will come again and receive you to*
> *Myself, that where I am, there you may be also* (John 14:2-3).

In His death and resurrection, Christ made a covenant with the Bride, betrothing us to Himself for eternity, and then left the Spirit of Truth with us to keep us pure and get us ready for His return. The Holy Spirit is waiting with us in great anticipation for the Groom's voice; this is why *"the Spirit and the bride say, 'Come'"* (Rev. 22:17)!

History culminates with a wedding, and we should celebrate this when we go to weddings and see all the ways they remind us of the great joy that awaits us. But that great wedding is only the beginning of an eternal marriage. For this reason, marriage is the pinnacle reflection of eternal relationships. Marriage is a glory-carrier, revealing the passionate commitment of Heaven to an agenda of endless love. Marriage is our tutor on the way to the marriage supper of the Lamb.

In the language of the apostle Paul, marriage is the interplay of love and submission. The many debates over the second word arise because of problems with the first. But when the love of husbands truly reflects Christ's love for the Church as Paul instructed (see Eph. 5:25), then wives experience the joy in submitting to their husbands that we experience in submitting our lives to Christ and entering into the safety and freedom of following His lead in life.

As I said before, we can only give what we have received. We cannot expect to love one another like Christ until we have learned to be loved by Him, to experience the reality of how He loves us. This is why the apostle Paul not only told us what our love is to look like, but also, in the same letter, prayed a powerful apostolic prayer for us to have *yada* of this love:

> *For this reason I bow my knees before the Father, from whom every family in heaven and on earth derives its name, that He would grant you, according to the riches of His glory, to be strengthened with power through His Spirit in the inner man, so that Christ may dwell in your hearts through faith; and that you, being rooted and grounded in love, may be able to comprehend with all the saints what is the breadth and length and height and depth, and to know the love of Christ which surpasses*

knowledge, that you may be filled up to all the fullness of God (Ephesians 3:14-19).

I believe that in this prayer we see the key to preserving marriages—seeking to know the love of Christ and falling on His power in our inner man to bring us into the fullness of that love.

The culture of divorce that has developed over the last half-century has been devastating to all of us, and restoring people who divorce is a vital ministry of the Church. But even as we see the ways people fall short of entering into God's design for marriage, we must not let go of the fact that lifelong marriage is the goal! I submit that we would do much in addressing the problem of bad marriages and divorce by spending more time looking at the love of Christ, and then at how right and beautiful marriage is when it expresses that love. There are couples among us who have celebrated as many as 60 or 70 years of covenant love together, love that has only grown stronger as it has weathered the ups and downs of life. Their lives are the greatest canvas displaying what the love of Jesus, our Groom, looks like, love that endures despite our betrayals and rebellions and love of other gods—love that is willing to shed its own blood. We must endeavor to keep this picture of marriage before us, for what we behold, we become!

In our independent culture, we often forget and therefore miss the advantages of the fact that marriage is also an adoption. The groom is adopted by his bride's parents and she by his. As a result of this connection, the children that result from their marriage are connected through their parents, not just to a chain of relationships, but to an entire tapestry of relationships through which, when they express the design of God, bring multiplied life and blessing to each generation.

Learning From Relationships

From the original marriage of Adam and Eve has come the rich design of the human family. Every legitimate human relationship was made with glory, with an eternal value because it reveals, points to, or reflects the attributes, nature, and power of God. Our relationships were made to reflect the relationships of the Trinity and our relationships with the Father, Son, and Holy Spirit. Every relationship we have is a highway or tutor through which we can learn something about Heaven and the Holy Trinity.

Relationships have been the arena where I have most clearly learned that you don't know what you don't know. If you, as I did, grew up without certain relationships, there will be dynamics of your growth you will need to learn later in life. For example, as I've watched those who have brothers, I've seen that in their rough and tumble, they learn to fight and still maintain love, skills that are essential in working on a team. I didn't know that I didn't know that and have often been afraid of conflict for this very reason.

The diversity of the relational aspects of God is reflected in the variety here on Earth. We are meant to have the capacity at any given time to be a father or mother, son or daughter, brother or sister, uncle, aunt, cousin, nephew, etc.—different relationships overlapping rather than graduating from one to the next. Every one of these has glory-carrying and glory-revealing capacity! We tend to think in a linear fashion, on a single track. We ask, "Who am I?" and we are looking for a single answer. But the truth is, on any given day I can come home and say, "I've been a husband today, I've been a father today, I've been a friend today, I've been a pastor today, I've been a coach today, and I've been a brother today." I carry all of that range of identities. It is a mistake to think that we must leave one type of relationship behind and move on to another. Our glorious assignment is to live in a multiplicity of relationships! And when we do, we reveal the relationships of Heaven! In all legitimate examples of God-designed relationships, we are able to experience and observe more of our relationship with God the Father, God the Son, and God the Holy Spirit, and they with each other. He wants us to experience relationships in all their fullness, for the more we do, the more we experience God and express His glory in our lives.

Chapter 8

WHAT IS MAN?

What is man, that You take thought of him…? (Psalm 8:4)

I N Psalm 8, David leads us into his own journey to discover the nature and purpose of mankind. He first looks up at God: *"O Lord, our Lord, how majestic is Your name in all the earth, who have displayed Your splendor above the heavens!"* (8:1). Then he looks up at what God has made: *"…I consider Your heavens, the work of Your fingers, the moon and the stars, which You have ordained"* (8:3). And then, in light of these realities, he asks: *"What is man that You take thought of him, and the son of man that You care for him?"* (8:4). These questions indicate, of course, David's knowledge that God does think of and care for mankind in a unique way, for He has given us a unique design and position in creation. Michelangelo captured man's uniqueness in his profound depiction of God and Adam on the ceiling of the Sistine Chapel. Of all the works God made with His finger, man is the only one with his finger reaching back to God. This certainly evokes the truth we've explored in the preceding chapters, that mankind was created in the image of God for relationship. But as David saw, we also reflect God's image as the delegated rulers of His creation. Thus, even as we look up at all the vast and incredible beauty of God's creation, we are also looking *down* at it from a special position:

> *You have made him a little lower than God, and You crown him*
> *with glory and majesty! You make him to rule over the works of*
> *Your hands; You have put all things under his feet, all sheep and*
> *oxen, and also the beasts of the field, the birds of the heavens and*
> *the fish of the sea, whatever passes through the paths of the seas*
> (Psalm 8:5-8).

David also saw that our commission originally declared to Adam and Eve to "rule over the works" of God (see Gen. 1:28) was given to mankind in addition to another commission: *"Out of the mouth of babes and nursing infants You have ordained strength, because of Your enemies, that You may silence the enemy and the avenger"* (Ps. 8:2 NKJV). The word translated *strength* here is also translated *praise* (NIV). Of all His works, God has given to mankind alone a power in our mouths, a power that reflects His own power to speak the worlds into existence. And this power is founded in our praise.

In designing human beings for relationship and dominion, God designed us to be worshipers. Whatever we worship shapes our worldview and shapes the world through us. It is for this reason that the apostle Paul identifies the Fall of Man, and the subsequent perversion of our relationship with the creation over which we were commissioned to rule, as a perversion of worship:

> *For even though they knew God, they did not honor Him as*
> *God or give thanks, but they became futile in their speculations,*
> *and their foolish heart was darkened. Professing to be wise, they*
> *became fools, and exchanged the glory of the incorruptible God*
> *for an image in the form of corruptible man and of birds and*
> *four-footed animals and crawling creatures. Therefore God gave*
> *them over in the lusts of their hearts to impurity, so that their*
> *bodies would be dishonored among them. For they exchanged*
> *the truth of God for a lie, and worshiped and served the crea-*
> *ture rather than the Creator, who is blessed forever...* (Romans
> 1:21-25).

The worship of man, exalting ourselves above God, was the sin that caused our Fall, and it is the sin we have walked in ever since. In our age, it is better known as *humanism*. The Greeks were the first to popularize humanism (Protagoras formulated his famous dictum, "Man is the measure of all things..."[1]), but the form of humanism that has influenced Western culture most directly grew up in the Renaissance. The Renaissance was one of the greatest seasons of man's creative ability, characterized by incredible art, architecture, medical knowledge, and music, which in so many instances (Michelangelo's Sistine Chapel being one of the greatest) pointed directly to God. Yet at that same time, men started pointing to each other and saying, "Look at what we can do. We don't need God." Instead of becoming enamored, as David was, with the works of God's hands, we became enamored with the works of our own hands. This pride has only grown in the West as we have continued to *praise* our superior power to engineer government and society and to build technologies by which to accomplish virtually anything.

Historically, humanist arguments have been used to defend and promote noble, humanitarian causes. But we must give heed to the powerful prophetic word Paul gave us in Romans 1:23 regarding where we inevitably end up when we allow humanism to define society and culture. When we put God below man, we exchange the "incorruptible" for the "corruptible," and this can only lead to our destruction. In fact, I submit that humanism is behind all the failed philosophies and destructive events of the past few centuries. Instead of promoting humanitarian causes, the humanism of the West has produced all the anti-human expressions of our age. It has led to tyranny and world wars, promoted abortion, distorted human rights, perverted the justice system, and rewritten the foundational laws of Christian nations.

The Church has long stood against the worship of man, calling it blasphemous and rightly pointing out its inevitably disastrous consequences. But Christians have also fallen into an equally blasphemous error by letting the pendulum swing, not from worshiping man to worshiping God, but to decrying man. Instead of breaking the spell of man's love for his own works by lifting his head to see the infinite beauty and greatness of God, we have pushed his face in the dirt. We've said, "We're just dust. We're just trash, not worth anything." These words not only defame us; they defame the Son of God who became a Man and paid the highest price to restore us to God. As Kris Vallotton likes to point out, the price God paid defines the value of what He purchased. To say we are worthless is to say the cross was meaningless.

The only real answer the Church can and must give to a society bound in the self-worship of humanism is to put the superior worship of God, and its superior results, on display. The true greatness and glory of mankind only rises to the surface when we align ourselves under the One who has given them to us, the One who is far greater and more glorious.

Our Restored Commission

According to Christ's words in John 17, He gave us His glory in order to make us one with Him and the Father. We've seen that this restoration to glory restored us to relationship with Him and one another. But this restoration was not merely a reconciliation. It was a recreation. In Christ, God created a new race of men and women who not only bear His image but also are *"partakers"* of His *"divine nature"* (2 Pet. 1:4). We are no longer children of the first Adam, who failed in his commission to subdue the earth. We now trace our bloodline to the last Adam, who conquered death itself and who, in making us to partake of His nature, has equipped us to finish the job He began of caring for and ruling over creation. Our glorious assignment as sons and daughters of God, Paul says, is to bring creation into the *"freedom of* [our] *glory"*:

> For the anxious longing of the creation waits eagerly for the revealing of the sons of God. For the creation was subjected to futility, not willingly, but because of Him who subjected it, in hope that the creation itself also will be set free from its slavery to corruption into the freedom of the glory of the children of God.

*For we know that the whole creation groans and suffers the pains
of childbirth together until now* (Romans 8:19-22).

You'll notice that Paul used the same terms here in Romans 8 that he used in Romans 1: When we became *"futile in* [our] *speculations"* and embraced the *"corruptible,"* creation *"was subjected to futility"* and entered *"slavery to corruption."* This reveals, in the negative, that God never revoked His mandated relationship between man and creation. When we fell, creation fell with us. Instead of being subdued, it was enslaved. But as we rise to take our rightful place of dominion in Christ, creation will rise with us. It will be restored to glory and reach the potential for expressing incredible richness and beauty it can only reach through our care and cultivation.

This promise should stir something in us and prompt questions. It should prompt us to follow in the psalmist's footsteps and take a fresh look at the world that we were made to rule, for when we truly look at creation, we will see both its beauty and its brokenness. We will feel both the wonder of its glorious reflection of the Creator and the pain of its "groaning" in captivity. And we will discover our glorious assignment right in the midst of this tension between what is and what ought to be.

Obviously, this assignment easily leads to the subject of environmentalism, and undoubtedly, the strongest argument for our responsibility to care for the earth is found here. But the more fundamental assignment is *worship.* This is where the psalmist began and ended his discovery of man's God-given identity and purpose, with an expression of worship: *"O Lord, our Lord, how majestic is Your name in all the earth...!"* (Ps. 8:1). We are to direct the power of praise in our mouths to the One who is worthy of praise, for when we do, His enemies are silenced, we are free to be who He created us to be, and creation experiences the restoration that only flows as God's sons and daughters delight in His works as they delight in Him.

What the Renaissance humanists and the generations following have missed is that the wonder and joy of human discovery and creativity actually reach their greatest heights when they are fueled by praise. So many people have wrongly thought that submitting our lives to God meant shutting down our gifts and abilities. The exact opposite is true. Submitting our lives to God in worship and walking in partnership with Him is the only way our gifts and abilities can function as they were designed, bringing us ultimate fulfillment and joy. The psalmist gives us the clue for seeing this truth by pointing us to "babes" and "infants." When children have a good father, the greatest pleasure they have is in pleasing him—in making things for him, in performing for him, in being with him. And nothing pleases a good father more than seeing the personalities, talents, and creativity of his children expressed. This is exactly the dynamic our Father has designed us to live from as worshipers and rulers.

The Treasure Hunt

I love this era in which we live. It is so full and so rich. I remember talking to my grandfather, Ernest Rayner, who died in 1987 at the age of 96, about the near century in which he lived. He was born before cars, once drove cattle across London Bridge, and died 20 years after man landed on the moon and the beautiful supersonic aircraft Concorde ruled the skies. He used to preach a message about what would happen when we ran out of oil for lamps. He saw the arrival of gas and electricity, and his message was fulfilled before his eyes: "The Lord will provide."

The beautiful thing is that most of how God has provided for this planet is by giving us insights, ideas, and knowledge that have enabled us to harness the resources that have always been available in creation. He wants to provide for needs, but even more, He wants us to grow up into our calling as stewards of the planet. In fact, the more we step into that assignment, the more we will gain access to all that the Lord has already provided for us to accomplish it. Every call of God comes fully equipped.

I sometimes amuse myself with the thought that God sits in the heavens and laughs (see Ps. 2:4). I wonder what He laughs at. I know I have taken this verse out of context, but I believe that the Lord is always laughing, not just to mock our silly arrogance, but also to delight in our discoveries and success. I think He laughs with the joyous laugh of a parent who watches a toddler's first steps and knows that one day he or she will run like the wind.

I realize that God is eternal and looks at history as a finished work that He Himself made. In this sense, there are no surprises for Him. And yet, I think we inherited our love of surprise from Him. The joy of looking back at a wild sky of storm clouds and seeing a rainbow, or of waking up to presents on Christmas morning, or of meeting the love of your life—that joy is just a drop of the great joy that God has in every moment of the story He has told. Precisely because He is eternal, He is able to be fully present in every moment and delight in it to the fullest.

To put it another way, God has set up history like a great treasure hunt. He says, *"It is the glory of God to conceal a matter, but the glory of kings is to search out a matter"* (Prov. 25:2). God has concealed a great matter for His sons and daughters to discover—the reality of His Kingdom—and the great surprise ending to the story is that His royal sons and daughters finally find the mother load. Thus, for God every moment of history is filled with the joy and excitement of the ending. He sees even in our stumbling baby steps, the beginnings of the glorious host of mature sons and daughters who will be just like Him and inherit all that He has. Every step we take to explore, invent, discover, and create delights Him.

From Hyde Park to Mammoth Lakes

There are two particular groups of people who have revealed to me the beauty and power that flows from our lives when our God-given creativity comes alive through the *strength* of praise. Both of these may seem strange examples for a man in his 50s. The first group is the rap and hip-hop generation. While I was running a young offender prison in Oxfordshire, England, I was contacted by two unlikely young men who wanted to minister in my prison using rap music. I had always been adventurous in trying to provide appropriate rehabilitative care for the prisoners, so I agreed for them to come in. On a Sunday morning, Watchman and Gifted began what became a two-year relationship with me and the young men in my care. This relationship culminated in my proudest career moment, as I stood at the back of a stage in front of 100,000 people at London's Hyde Park and watched four young men called the XKONZ (graduates of Watchman and Gifted's rap academy) perform, "We Can Kick It! Yes We Can!"

I believe that God has always had a purpose for this genre of music. He knew a generation would arise that would not have their eyes drawn to Heaven by Wesley or Handel. They would find another sound, another rhythm. Just because rap has been used to convey hatred is no reason to dismiss it; rather, it is reason to redeem it for divine purpose. With tongue in cheek, I kept the biography of Tupac Shakur on my office desk because I love what he said:

> If we're all saying that rap is an artform then we gotta be more responsible for our lyrics. If you see everybody dying because of what you're saying, it don't matter that you didn't make them die, it just matters that you didn't save them.[2]

Watchman and Gifted ran a rap academy for me with two rules—no obscene language and only positive messages. They demonstrated that this genre of music could be used to benefit the young men in my care and in some cases connect them with God. They left a mark on my life, and so did the XKONZ. It is a mark that I hope will always allow me to believe and see that the next genre, the next style, is an opportunity for man to continue the unfolding of his mastery of this planet and use it to bring glory to God.

The second group is the snowboarders. My contact with this community began with a little church in Mammoth Lakes, California, that attended a supernatural strategic planning workshop I led. At the end of that week, the teams presented their plans. This church had a plan to lead people to the Lord on the mountain slopes, board with them, and disciple them with a vision that one day they would send these disciples to the mountains of the world. Six months later, they had started a church in New Zealand and now have churches in Switzerland and Canada.

They have become my friends, and through them I have seen how snowboarding, though a sport only just over 30 years old, has captured the hearts of a generation. When coupled with a love for God, the sense of adventure, the delight in nature, and the sheer love of life that snowboarders carry is full of Kingdom potential.

Amongst this extraordinary group is a heroine truly taking the opportunities of this era, living to the max, and not living to please man but God. Her name is Kelly Clark. She is the 2002 USA Olympic Half Pipe gold medalist and 2010 bronze medalist, but you are as likely to find her worshiping God in the church in Mammoth as doing her stuff on the greatest slopes of the world. She has taken an opportunity, a new sport, with one goal in mind—to use her skill in mastering the slopes and the board to point people to God. Her snowboard, seen worldwide at the Vancouver Olympics, bears a message declaring her life of praise: "Jesus, I cannot hide my love."

Restoring Truth

Watchman wrote a great song with this line in it: "God created monkey; monkey did not make man." It is my absolute favorite. The myth of evolution (as opposed to the scientific theory) and the materialistic view of the universe it is used to support are two of the many lies that humanism has exchanged with *the truth of God* in order to sustain the worship of man. But embracing these lies has invited the insanity and illness that always comes from living in a contradiction. Erasing the supernatural from reality (materialism) has left us with a vision of the universe that is simultaneously far more fantastic and far less wonderful than believing that it was made by a Creator. I love to watch nature programs, and when I do, I sit and think,

You have to have a lot more faith than I have to believe that the incredible array of animals on this planet came from anywhere other than the Creator God. It takes more faith than I think probably all of us have got together. And all that faith in biology never enlarges the world, as seeing God exalted above the heavens did for David. It only shrinks it and reduces it to mere mechanical processes.

It is time for the sons and daughters of God to bring sanity and wonder to the world's vision of themselves and creation through their lives of praise. We have to show them how right and how amazing the world is and how glorious and creative we are when God is on His throne and we are His beloved children training to rule and reign with Him for eternity. In displaying the true image and substance of God's divine nature as worshipers and stewards of creation, we will expose the false image of "corruptible man" for what it is and invite men and women to discover who they really are and why they are on the planet.

What is man? We are God's idea, God's expression, and God's family delegates here on Earth. We bear His image, share His substance, are filled with His Spirit, have the mind of Christ, and carry Christ, the hope of glory, within us. How can we be ourselves except by living to praise Him?

Endnotes

1. *Dictionary.com* Cultural Dictionary, s.v. "man is the measure of all things," http://dictionary.reference.com/browse/Man+is+the+measure+of+all+things; accessed January 30, 2011.

2. Alan Light, *Tupac Shakur* (London: Plexus Publishing, 1997), 46.

Chapter 9

BEAUTY AND GLORY

Never lose an opportunity of seeing anything beautiful, for beauty is God's handwriting.

—Ralph Waldo Emerson

OUR Glorious assignment as sons and daughters begins and ends with worship. Fittingly, the story of Moses and the Israelites, which foreshadows our restoration to glory, also foreshadows this assignment. After the Lord delivered Israel, brought them safely to the mountain, and received their promise to obey the Ten Commandments, He had one thing on His agenda. He called Moses to a 40-day summit meeting to discuss His plan for establishing a house of worship among His people. Only when the foundation of worship had been laid in their lives could God's people embark on their divine mission.

We can only try to imagine what this meeting on the mountain, in which God revealed the plan for the Tabernacle, must have been like for Moses. The Bible doesn't give us many details, but one thing it does indicate is that Moses was not just hearing the Lord describe the intricate details of each aspect of His house. He was seeing a "pattern" of these things.

> *Let them construct a sanctuary for Me, that I may dwell among them. According to all that I am going to show you, as the*

*pattern of the tabernacle and the pattern of all its furniture, just
so you shall construct it* (Exodus 25:8-9).

The writer of Hebrews, in showing how the provisional ministry of the
Old Covenant was fulfilled in the New, provides us with more information
about this pattern:

*Now the main point in what has been said is this: we have
such a high priest, who has taken His seat at the right hand
of the throne of the Majesty in the heavens, a minister in the
sanctuary and in the true tabernacle, which the Lord pitched,
not man. For every high priest is appointed to offer both gifts
and sacrifices; so it is necessary that this high priest also have
something to offer. Now if He were on earth, He would not be
a priest at all, since there are those who offer the gifts according to the Law; who serve a copy and shadow of the heavenly
things, just as Moses was warned by God when he was about
to erect the tabernacle; for, "see," he says, "that you make all
things according to the pattern which was shown you on the
mountain"* (Hebrews 8:1-5).

These verses suggest something astounding, something that expands
even further our earlier list of all that Moses saw preceding his audacious
request to see even more. God showed Moses the *"pattern"* for the Tabernacle by unveiling the *"heavenly things,"* the eternal realities, the Tabernacle
would represent. Moses actually saw the throne room of God.

It is not my purpose here to dig into Exodus and Hebrews and thor-
oughly unpack the rich symbolism of the furniture in the Tabernacle and the
stunning realities they point to. I'll only remind you again that everything
Moses saw in receiving the Old Covenant was a promise for us as believers
in the New Covenant. When Jesus told the woman at the well that God
sought worshipers who worship Him *"in spirit and truth"* (John 4:24), He

was referring to the fulfillment of this promise. We worship in spirit and in truth in the New Covenant because we now participate directly in the heavenly realities Moses witnessed, and no longer with their earthly symbols.

What I do want to look at is what God said after He described the house He wanted His people to build for Him. The next thing on God's list was what the men serving in that house were to wear. As with the items in the Tabernacle, every aspect of the priests' garments had design, purpose, and meaning associated with their ministry. The ephod, breastplate, and headpiece were worn only by the high priest, for these items were related to his unique role as the intercessor who went into the Holy of Holies on the Day of Atonement. They all point to the ministry of Christ, who, as Hebrews explains, entered the actual Holy of Holies in Heaven and presented Himself as the atoning sacrifice for our sins once and for all (see Heb. 9:11-14). But the high priest's garments and the garments of "Aaron's sons" had something in common that tells us about the nature of our ministry as members of a *"royal priesthood"* (1 Pet. 2:9):

> [And God says] *You shall make holy garments for Aaron your brother, for glory and for beauty...*[and] *for Aaron's sons you shall make tunics; you shall also make sashes for them, and you shall make caps for them, for glory and for beauty* (Exodus 28:2,40).

The men who served in God's house were to be clothed in *glory* and *beauty*. And when we look at what their clothing was made of, we learn more about what this means. The priests' garments were made from the same materials as the Tabernacle:

> *Moreover you shall make the tabernacle with ten curtains of fine twisted linen and blue and purple and scarlet material...* (Exodus 26:1).

...they shall make holy garments for Aaron your brother and his sons, that he may minister as priest to Me. They shall take the gold and the blue and the purple and the scarlet material and the fine linen (Exodus 28:4-5).

The glory and beauty of the priests' garments was the glory and beauty of the house of God. God wanted them to be a reflection of what they were seeing and touching. Even more—He wanted them to be part of it.

Moses and Royalty

Throughout the Bible, the materials used for the Tabernacle and the priests' garments are unmistakably connected to *royalty*. When Pharaoh promoted Joseph to royal status, he *"clothed him in garments of fine linen and put the gold necklace around his neck"* (Gen. 41:42). When King Ahasuerus promoted Mordecai to prime minister:

Then Mordecai went out from the presence of the king in royal robes of blue and white, with a large crown of gold and a garment of fine linen and purple... (Esther 8:15).

When God promoted Israel to be His chosen people, He did the same, as He told them through the prophet Ezekiel:

Thus you were adorned with gold and silver, and your dress was of fine linen, silk and embroidered cloth...so you were exceedingly beautiful and advanced to royalty (Ezekiel 16:13).

And finally, when we celebrate our ultimate promotion as the Bride of Christ at the marriage of the Lamb, we will wear *"fine linen"* (Rev. 19:8).

These materials show us that the Tabernacle was more than a sanctuary; it was a King's house. And the only person in Israel who had ever lived in a king's house was Moses. If God had wanted a brick house, of course, it would have been easy. The Israelites knew about bricks—how to gather the straw, gather the clay, dry the bricks, cook the bricks, and make the bricks probably any shape you could possibly imagine. They were experts in bricks. But God wanted a house fit for royalty. He needed a man who understood and appreciated royal things. Moses had protested that God had the wrong guy, but the truth was that he wasn't just the right guy; he was the only guy. Even though it had been a while since he was in Pharaoh's house, Moses undoubtedly remembered his days of finer living. Have you ever been with people who have been brought up on the fine things in life, but who have fallen into hard times? If you go with them to a high-class store or restaurant, they just step straight back in. A cultivated palate for gourmet food or wine doesn't go away.

On the other hand, the very term *cultivated* indicates that good taste doesn't come naturally. It must be developed through training. Moses' training in Pharaoh's house prepared him to see and appreciate the extravagant vision and description God gave him on the mountain. It not only prepared him to see it so that he could oversee its construction and make sure everything was made according to the "pattern." It prepared him to see the revelation of the kind of King the Lord was, how He intended to draw these former slaves into relationship with Him, and how Moses was to lead them into that relationship.

I also believe that seeing God's beauty awakened an attraction in Moses that prepared him to ask his audacious question for more—it drew him toward greater intimacy, *yada*, with God. In fact, this is the nature of beauty. *Beauty is an attraction of the soul that invites intimacy.* If you don't think that is true, ask a man who just recently fell in love with a woman. He saw beauty, which attracted him and became an invitation to intimacy, to know the beautiful person more. This attraction is precisely why God wanted His house and His priests to be beautiful. God wants His people to share in His beauty for the sake of relationship. He wanted us to be drawn to Him and Himself to us.

But how do we see beauty? The maxim "beauty is in the eye of the beholder" tells us something about how we relate to beauty. It doesn't mean that the beholder imparts beauty to what he sees; it means that beauty is something we can only perceive according to the state of our faculty of perception. We see what we are prepared to see. This is why God couldn't take any Israelite to the mountain and show him the *"heavenly things"* of His throne room. Without some level of ability to perceive and appreciate royal things, they would be completely alien, unintelligible.

So, just as God used Moses to reveal His goodness to Israel and train them to walk according to its standard, so God used Moses to reveal His beauty and train them to see it. His faithfulness to "make everything according to the pattern" allowed the people to be exposed, on a regular basis, to royal beauty. This exposure gathered momentum with each generation, until finally a man was born who was so captivated by the beauty of God that he broke into a realm of *yada* unparalleled by any other Old Testament figure.

Beholding Beauty

This man, of course, was David, the consummate worshiper in the Bible. He said:

> One thing I have desired of the Lord, that will I seek: that I may dwell in the house of the Lord all the days of my life, to behold the beauty of the Lord, and to inquire in His temple (Psalm 27:4 NKJV).

Notice that David uses the word *temple*. Seeing as there was no temple in Israel until his son Solomon built one, we know that David was speaking about something else. I suggest that David saw, in some measure, the ultimate plan of God to bring His sons and daughters to live in His very presence—in the *"true tabernacle."* The very next verse says, *"In the secret place of His tabernacle He shall hide me"* (Ps. 27:5). If he didn't see that this was the plan, he at least saw that it was available for him and that he had to have it.

He was so attracted by God's beauty that he pursued the invitation to intimacy right past all the protocols that God had Moses set up. He didn't want the copies; he wanted the *"heavenly things."*

David understood the principle God had revealed by clothing His priests in the same glory and beauty as the Tabernacle in which they served. God wanted His people to see that they would become like what they beheld. But He also wanted them to see that the beauty of the Tabernacle was only a sign pointing to the beauty of God Himself. Only those who allowed the beauty of God's house to attract them to relationship with God, as David did, would discover His unfathomable, endlessly faceted beauty. And the result of beholding this beauty was something far deeper than cultivating a taste for the external trappings of royalty. Beholding the beauty of God cultivated David's taste for being like God.

Becoming like God is the fruit of worship. In worship, we behold the beauty of God, which awakens our attraction to Him, invites us to know Him, and rouses us to *"inquire"* of Him. Beauty always raises questions. For the man in love, it often raises the question, "Will you marry me?" The man who asks this question—we hope—asks it because he has met someone he wants to spend a lifetime getting to know. And if he spends that lifetime getting to know her, and she him, they will increasingly express the reality that "two become one." They'll finish each other's sentences. They'll think alike. They'll be in tune with each other. This is the likeness, the oneness, that God invites us to grow into with Him through a lifetime of beholding Him in worship. This is what He invites us to with His beauty.

Dwelling in the House of the Lord

There is just as much danger of becoming religious in a renewal church as anywhere else. That might seem scary, but plenty of people have attempted to adopt David's *"one thing"* as their "one thing" and have developed a religious routine or some other unsustainable plan for "dwelling in the house of the Lord all the days of their lives." It simply can't mean living at church.

Some of us are privileged to spend a large amount of our week at church, and honestly, it is the privilege of my life. I say to people, "I am a man who lives on vacation and gets paid to go to church." It is a great way of life. But church is not the house the psalmist was talking about. He was talking about God's tabernacle—the *"true tabernacle"* in Heaven.

In the New Covenant, we live in this great mystery: we are both seated in Christ in heavenly places, where we can come boldly before the throne of grace, and we are also the dwelling place of God on Earth, the temple of the Holy Spirit (see Eph. 2:6; Heb. 4:16; 1 Cor. 6:19). We worship God in Heaven and not in a building and yet the Kingdom of Heaven is within us (see Luke 17:21). Thus, entering into the psalmist's *"one thing"* means learning to live, in every situation, season, and relationship, in the reality that we live in Him and He lives in us. It means that we are to learn to behold His beauty and inquire of Him in every part of our lives. It means training ourselves to see Him in all of life so that we can see life as it really is and relate to it as His glorious sons and daughters. The sign that we are doing this is that our attraction to God, to all that He is and all He has made, grows and is expressed.

There is a beautiful mountain near us in Redding—Mount Shasta. Sue and I love living surrounded by mountains. We used to live in Windsor, just west of London. It is pretty flat, with a lot of buildings, little open space, and definitely no mountains. When I look at Mount Shasta, it awakens a desire in me. I want to photograph it—from every angle, in every light, with every type of cloud around it. The beauty of the mountain invites me to come and know it, but to come to know it in a way that is unique to me. I know others who, when they look at the mountain, want to get to know it in other ways. The snowboarders want to snowboard it. The climbers want to climb it. Geologists and seismologists want to study it. Artists want to paint it.

It's the same with the ocean. Some people want to surf it. Others want to sail it, fish in it, travel on it, dive in it, and study what's underneath. Others want to paint it or photograph it. Its beauty attracts us differently because we are all different. God designed us this way. He clothed each of us in various facets of His beauty. When we encounter His beauty and are attracted to it, we express that attraction in different ways, and this draws out His beauty in us.

I believe our diverse attractions to beauty have sparked most of the creative energy and endeavors throughout history. They have taken people to the depths of the ocean and far into space. But wherever this attraction has not led to the worship of the Creator, it has further led to abuse and neglect of creation and each other. We must recognize that the attraction we feel to mountains, or the sea, or insects, or architecture, or music, is really an attraction to the One who made them. He wants us to follow our desires to their source, and inquire of Him: "God, who are You? How did You make that? Why did You make it that way? What does that mountain tell me about You? What does that eagle soaring tell me about You? And why I am so drawn to these things? What does this tell me about how You made me? What do You want me to do about it?"

This inquiry is the treasure hunt I spoke of in the last chapter. Each of us is a king whose glory will rise to the surface as we search out the matters God has hidden for us. And beauty is what motivates this search.

Displaying His Beauty

I recently bought the BBC series *Planet Earth*. It is just amazing. I don't have any words to describe it. It brings tears to your eyes to watch this program, which was filmed over five years and explores the jungles, deserts, forests, deep oceans, shallow seas, and every other area of this incredible planet. It is wonderful to watch the behavior of animals—a shark that gives 500 liters a day of milk to its baby, and yet is starving itself because it is waiting to find food, or a penguin that stores one meal for its chick when it comes out. It's wonderful to see what lives in the deepest parts of the sea or how a forest begins to return to life virtually within a day after a forest fire. It is beautiful—so, so beautiful. And all its beauty reveals the beauty of the One who made it.

Healing is beautiful. Maybe you haven't thought of it that way. Have you ever looked at your hand when you cut yourself and seen how it heals over? It is beautiful. God made it that way. He programmed us to get well. This is actually the fundamental truth behind creative miracles, which are also beautiful. Souls getting saved are beautiful. Weddings are beautiful. A man loving a woman for life, having kids and grandkids, being a family, and leaving a legacy—that is beautiful.

What attracts you? What touches you? What awakens in your heart when you behold the beauty of God? I think we need to give ourselves greater permission, particularly when we are before God in worship in a church service or in our own devotional life with the Lord, to let our minds wander to the universe, to the mountains, to healings—to beauty. Don't be surprised when creative ideas start flooding your mind in worship. Many of us have experienced this and shut it down, thinking it was a distraction. We need to learn to distinguish between distractions and the Lord awakening our hearts. We should expect that in the beautiful presence of God, which is magnified in corporate worship, our own priestly beauty is going to come out; the ideas and desires that are actually His glory in us will begin to come out and be expressed.

We also need to stop comparing and disqualifying ourselves because we aren't attracted to the same things and don't have the same beauty as the next person. Actually, we do have the same beauty—as sons and daughters, we are all clothed in the royal priestly robes of Heaven and share its beauty. But that beauty is so rich and diverse that God needs all of us to display different aspects and dimensions of it. As we learn to behold the beauty of the Lord and grow in the intimacy to which it draws us, we will no longer feel threatened by what other people have and instead appreciate it. We will also discover our own beauty and begin to put it on display.

I believe that God's plan is to win the world through the beauty of His priests. The reason that intimidating people with hell and torment is a limited motivational tool to bring people to God is because they were created to be attracted to beauty and repelled by the ugly. As Jesus prayed in John 17, it's our oneness with God, it's the fact that God's sons and daughters display His glory and beauty on their faces and in their lives, that brings the world to faith; that attracts them to know Him. As we learn to put His beauty on display, we will expose the world to the beauty of Heaven and eventually captivate entire nations with a desire to know the Beautiful One.

So pay attention to the things that attract you. If you pursue them to their Source, I believe you will be invited into your priestly ministry on the planet, into the specific assignment God has for you to partner with Him in revealing His beauty. I can't wait to see what will happen when an entire company of people, a generation, begins to see, pursue, and carry this beauty. As believers, we have so much, and yet we have tapped into so little. We have four times the resources of the most successful unbelievers in our society. They are made in the image of God, as we are. But we are filled with the Spirit, we have Christ in us, the hope of glory, and we have the mind of Christ. We have direct access to the One who created the universe, and His promise to impart His divine wisdom for subduing the earth by guiding us into all truth (see John 16:13). I think it's time that the Church became the greatest, most attractive organization of the planet.

But we must always remember that attracting the world is the by-product, not the goal, of worship. The goal of worship is to attract the King. Like every pure bride, the Bride of Christ reserves her beauty and her glory for her Husband alone. And when He is truly the *"one thing"* we desire, then, like every ardent bridegroom, He will not be able to stay away.

> *Listen, O daughter, consider and incline your ear; forget your own people also, and your father's house; so the King will greatly desire your beauty; because He is your Lord, worship Him...*

The royal daughter is all glorious within the palace; her clothing is woven with gold (Psalm 45:10-11,13 NKJV).

Chapter 10

HONOR

No person was ever honored for what he receives. Honor has been the reward for what he gave.

—Calvin Coolidge

JESUS Showed us that glory is revealed relationally. He brought us into His relationship with the Father, and in and through that relationship, we come to know a glory that makes the glory Moses knew look glory-less. He also modeled the mode of that relationship, which is honor. *Honor is both the desire and the ability to recognize glory in others.* (*Kabod*, the Hebrew word for glory, is translated "honor" 32 times in the Old Testament.[1]) Whenever I recognize in someone or something the attributes, nature, or power of God, I am beginning the journey of honoring. Put another way, honor is when I show value for something because it reveals, reflects, or points to the nature, attributes, or power of God.

The Revelation of Honor in the Cross

The cross is the supreme revelation of honor. At the cross, Jesus showed us how much He valued every man, woman, and child who ever has been and ever will be, and that includes the most heinous perpetrators of evil. He valued all of us above His own life. Why did Jesus value us so highly? And how could He recognize glory in us when we had fallen short of His glory? The answer to both questions is that Jesus recognized our eternal value and glory. He knew His Father's plan to "bring many sons to glory" (see Heb. 2:10) and saw all of us, despite the Fall, as the sons and daughters His Father had created for that purpose.

But of course, there is more to it. The word *recognize* is a little lacking because it suggests that Christ saw something in us that we already possessed. And we do possess it in eternity, but only because He gave it to us by dying on our behalf. Christ honored us through His death because it was only by His death that we could be made honorable. In showing how He valued us, He gave us that value.

Moreover, Christ's death did not merely restore the value that we lost in the Fall. The price God paid to redeem us was much greater than the price He paid to create us, and thus redeemed humanity is worth far more and has a far greater glory than Adam and Eve ever had in their innocence. When Christ restored us to glory (see John 17:22), Christ did not make us like Adam and Eve, but like Himself. In fact, He made us part of Himself. We are now members of a new divine-human race in Him, partaking in the divine nature in a way we never did as those merely made in the image of God.

The act by which Christ made us "new creations" forever defined how we are to relate to one another as people of such great value. Paul tells us that this supreme act of honor was the supreme act of humility:

> ...*Christ Jesus, who, although He existed in the form of God, did not regard equality with God a thing to be grasped, but emptied Himself, taking the form of a bond-servant, and being made in the likeness of men. Being found in appearance as a man, He humbled Himself by becoming obedient to the point of death, even death on a cross (Philippians 2:5-8).*

It seems humble enough that God became a Man. But that was only the starting point. Paul says He was already in appearance as a man, and *then* He humbled Himself—to the point of death. In His death, Jesus took a place below the worst of sinners, below an entire race of sinners. He humbled Himself to the lowest point and from that point He looked up because in complete and perfect humility the only place that you can look is up. But it was precisely getting to the bottom of things that positioned Christ to govern them.

One Saturday, while working as the in-charge governor (warden) in a young offenders' prison, I visited the segregation unit ("the hole" here in America). Prison is where the bad guys go, and segregation units are where the really bad guys go. On this occasion, a young man was brought down in arm locks to the unit by three big, burly officers. As they had been trained to do, the officers put him facedown in a stripped-out cell in the segregation unit. The normal procedure was to have men stationed at the prisoner's arms, legs, and head. One by one, each man would let go of a body part and retreat from the cell so nobody, including the prisoner, got hurt.

On this occasion, I walked into the cell and despite appearances, had an awareness of what was really going on with this young man. I knew he was more scared than dangerous. As the governor, what I said went, so I usually didn't say things unless I felt really confident about them.

"Let him go," I said.

"Do you know what you're doing?"

"Yes, let him go."

I sat on the floor next to him as they let him go. When I got down on his level, I saw things from his perspective. Four six-foot prison officers towered above us. It was very scary. I am much less physically imposing, especially when I'm on the ground. But even though I was on the ground, I was still the governor. From that position, I began to talk with that young man and govern the situation. I gave him the opportunity to trust me, an authority figure who had seen the world through his eyes. When I visited him on subsequent days, I found that my actions had created a pathway for a relationship founded on trust and understanding, rather than assumptions based on his previous experiences at the hands of authority figures.

This memory came to mind as I was meditating on the humility of Jesus. Jesus came down to our level, and then got lower still by serving us, first in His ministry and then in His death, where He *"descended into the lower parts of the earth"* (Eph. 4:9). He found the utmost depth to which humanity had fallen in sin and death and got below that. He saw things from our perspective; in fact, He saw them better, for He not only felt our brokenness but He also carried its full weight. But even as He identified fully with the consequences of our sin, He never lost His right or ability to govern. He governed from below, not above. He got below us in order to lift us up.

It may seem paradoxical to say that Christ humbled Himself in order to be exalted, but this is the truth Christ declared to us: *"…whoever humbles himself shall be exalted"* (Matt. 23:12). Paul tells us that this is precisely the formula at work in the cross: *"…He humbled Himself by becoming obedient to the point of death, even death on a cross. For this reason also, God highly exalted Him…"* (Phil. 2:8-9). But Jesus' humility and exaltation were entirely undertaken on our behalf. His journey to the lowest place was solely to obtain the thing we needed from God and couldn't get ourselves: grace.

One of the immutable aspects of God's character, like the fact that He is perfectly good, is this: *"God is opposed to the proud, but gives grace to the humble"* (James 4:6; 1 Pet. 5:5). Because of pride, we were disqualified from grace. But God found a way to give us the one thing that would restore us without violating His character, and it happens to be the same way He found to give us His glory. As we saw in Chapter 3, God did for the Son of Man what He hadn't been able to do for Moses. He could answer Jesus' request for glory because Jesus was not "another." Similarly, the grace He could not give to a humanity fallen in pride, He could give to His Son, who humbled Himself.

But in order to receive the full measure of grace needed by sinners, Christ had to identify with us completely. To identify with those dead in sin, He had to die. And because He identified with us fully, His death became our death. As Paul said, *"...one died for all, therefore all died"* (2 Cor. 5:14). At the cross, we were no longer dead in our sin; we were dead in Christ. And because we died with Him, we rose with Him when His Father raised Him from the dead:

> But God, being rich in mercy, because of His great love with which He loved us, even when we were dead in our transgressions, made us alive together with Christ (by grace you have been saved), and raised us up with Him, and seated us with Him in the heavenly places in Christ Jesus, so that in the ages to come He might show the surpassing riches of His grace in kindness toward us in Christ Jesus (Ephesians 2:4-7).

Christ went from the lowest place of humility to the highest place of honor, and He took us with Him by the power of grace. He elevated us to the position we were created to hold as the glorious sons and daughters of the King of kings and Lord of lords.

Honor Brings Life

Paul told us clearly what we were to make of this great drama, this grand gesture of God descending into humanity and into death, and then ascending with humanity to life. He said:

> Do nothing from selfishness or empty conceit, but with humility of mind regard one another as more important than yourselves; do not merely look out for your own personal interests, but also for the interests of others (Philippians 2:3-4).

Once again, the honor Christ paid us at the cross established the pattern of honor that defines the way we are to treat one another. The journey of honor requires first that we learn to value one another according to the value Christ has given us, and second that we learn to show that value as Christ did, by "[looking] out...for the interests of others" and treating them as more important than ourselves. We are all called to become "the slave [or servant] of all" (Mark 10:44), to take the low position in order to lift up those around us.

Throughout my tenure as a prison governor, I consistently sought ways of "getting under" the prisoners. For two years, I didn't allow a prisoner to come into my prison without first sitting down and talking to me for 15 minutes. It was a little unusual, but was something I really felt I should do. In that time, I interviewed at least 300 prisoners. I'd begin the interviews by saying, "I don't want to talk about your crime. By the time you've got to me, you've told your parents, your probation officer, about ten lawyers, three courts, the police, the two prisons you've been transferred into, and just about everybody about your crime. I want to talk about you. What do you love to do? What's the best thing that's ever happened to you? What vacation do you remember with your family? What would you like to do or achieve while you're in prison?"

Some of them just did not know how to answer. They were so shocked that I was taking an interest in them. They'd start telling me about their crimes, and I'd say, "I don't want to know about that." They'd say, "I'm doing six years," and I'd say, "I know you're doing six years. That's not the issue. I want to know about you. I want to get to know you."

At the time, the Board of Visitors Watchdog Committee used to do a group interview with all of the prisoners after they had seen me. One day, this lovely lady from the committee, Andrea, came down to see me. She said, "Paul, you've got a problem."

I said, "What do you mean I've got a problem?"

She said, "Those prisoners, they think you really like them."

"Actually, you're wrong," I said. "I don't like them; I love them."

I was determined to be a voice of honor in the lives of these young men, to show value for them on the basis of who God said they were, and not on the basis of their bad choices. I was determined to recognize the glory in them, no matter how buried it was. And I watched as many of these young men, in various ways, began to show signs of life. After that initial interview, many of them wanted to keep me updated on their progress. When I visited them in art room, workshop, or gymnasium, they were eager to share their achievements and successes with me.

Honor brings life. We see this most dramatically at the cross, where Christ's honor brought eternal, abundant life to the entire human race. But God first revealed this principle to Moses centuries earlier in the Fifth Commandment. He said, *"Honor your father and your mother, that your days may be prolonged in the land which the Lord your God gives you"* (Exod. 20:12). As I described earlier, reconnecting to my father by restoring my value for him caused many things to begin to come to life in me. Honor opened the artery of sonship, and since that time, I have been receiving nourishment that has affected my life, my family, and my future.

Even when our parents are gone, carrying an attitude of honor in our hearts and minds positions us to receive life from them. And this principle of honor extends to encounters with all people, for though our immediate family bonds are closest and therefore the most life-giving, the honor Christ paid to all of us made us a family and worthy of honor. This creates the potential for an exchange of life every time we interact with people and recognize Christ's value for them—even those who don't yet know Him, just as Christ recognized our value before we knew Him. And again, simply carrying honor in our hearts brings life even when we aren't interacting with people directly. Scripture teaches us to honor those in authority, for example, because even if we never speak to the president or prime minister, serving them through our prayers will promote life and peace in their sphere of influence (see Rom. 13:1-7; 1 Tim. 2:1-2).

The principle of honor also works in the negative, however. Scripture is clear that while honor, which is preceded by humility, brings life, dishonor, which is preceded by pride, cuts off life. Proverbs 18:12 says, *"Before destruction the heart of man is haughty, but humility goes before honor."* I like to illustrate this principle with a cooking example because I love to cook and collect recipes. (At eight years old, I started watching the Galloping Gourmet, one of the early celebrity chefs, and cooking meals for my parents, who ran a small grocery store and thus gave me access to a wide variety of ingredients. I must say that they, and later my wife, approved of my success in producing the Galloping Gourmet's dishes, but were less thrilled by my equal success in adopting his rather messy style in the kitchen!)

Imagine I am a famous chef visiting the home of a great cook. I'm confident I would never do this, but let's say that after she places her painstakingly prepared dessert on the table, I instantly tell her how much better my version of her dessert is. Her hopes of pleasing me are crushed. Trying to hide her disappointment, she laughs it off, serving me a piece with apologies that it hasn't passed muster. Pigheadedly, I continue to point out what her work lacks with each bite, until, abruptly, I'm interrupted. I look down and see that I am now wearing the dessert, and the cook is standing at the door waiting for me to vacate the premises. The dishonor produced by my pride has cut both of us off from all beneficial exchange and instead produced destruction.

But now imagine what might happen if I come to the cook's house in disguise. As she places her dessert on the table, I gasp at the sight and express how wonderful the aroma is. She serves me a portion and I, after savoring a few bites, pour out generous compliments about this unparalleled creation. Flattered, the cook begins to tell me the history of this great dessert—it is her great grandmother's recipe, brought with her family when they immigrated. She gets up from the table and pulls her scrapbook of recipes down from a shelf, along with a photo of her great-grandmother. I am impressed by what is, to my trained eye, a valuable cache of rare and special recipes. So at this point, I reveal my identity, tell her that I think she has a recipe book waiting to be published, and offer to help launch her in this venture.

In this scenario, humility preceded honor, and honor produced life. And what was that life? Clearly the enjoyment and nourishment of an excellent dessert was just a small part of it. The real treasure honor exposed was the excellence of the cook and her family. It made room for more of her greatness to come to life.

Glory to Glory by Honor

At Bethel, we have been working to develop a culture of honor, a culture where we call out the greatness, the "gold," in one another. We have embraced the Kingdom principle that the quality of life in our community is determined by how successful we are at recognizing the glory in others and issuing regular invitations for that glory to be expressed. Encouraging words have become common currency. You don't have to stick around Bethel very long before someone is telling you about the glory he or she sees in you. As a result, people all around us are coming to life in countless ways. It's miraculous.

However, as we have sought to establish honor in our lives, we have learned something important. As I said in the last chapter, we see what we are prepared to see. Recognizing the glory in others is not something we do automatically. We must train ourselves to see it, and we do this by training our minds to agree with the truth of how Christ has defined the value of the human race. This process of training our minds is what the Bible calls *repentance*. The Greek word for repentance, *metanoia*, means "to change one's mind"[2] or change the way you think. Only when our minds have embraced the revelation of our own glory and the glory of others will we be able to behave honorably. But in order to embrace this revelation, our minds are going to have to give up the wrong beliefs we've had about one another. This is where the real battle of faith is, the battle of trusting an unseen, eternal reality and letting it transform the way we negotiate visible, temporal reality, where we still obviously see, in ourselves and in everyone around us, how little we look like our Elder Brother.

Changing the way we think about one another is not an easy task in our current cultural climate, which is distinctly dishonoring, particularly in the popular attitude toward authority. When I was a young man at school, I did whatever the park keeper or anyone in a uniform told me to do because it was still normal to honor position and authority. Now it is normal to mock, criticize, and disobey those in authority, whether they are our parents or the president. Again, the root of dishonor is pride. We have arrogantly set ourselves up to judge and criticize everyone and anyone, regardless of their title or position. Jesus described us perfectly when He taught us not to judge:

> Do not judge so that you will not be judged. For in the way you judge, you will be judged; and by your standard of measure, it will be measured to you. Why do you look at the speck that is in your brother's eye, but do not notice the log that is in your own eye? Or how can you say to your brother, "Let me take the speck out of your eye," and behold, the log is in your own eye? You hypocrite, first take the log out of your own eye, and then you will see clearly to take the speck out of your brother's eye (Matthew 7:1-5).

With great logs of pride in our eyes, we simply cannot see people around us as they truly are. And the more we judge one another, the more we invite judgment on ourselves, for that's how judgment works. The result has been a downward spiral of greatness and an increase in lawlessness in our culture. Most everyone I took care of in prison was under the influence of this dishonoring, anti-authority attitude, and it had assiduously destroyed their lives.

But judgment also works in the positive direction. In fact, the core of honor is proper judgment—the just appraisal of the glory of others. When we, through repentance and humility, remove the logs from our eyes, then we can *"see clearly"* and help others to see clearly. When we treat others as more important than ourselves, when we measure their glory above our own, then we position ourselves to be measured by the same standard. The result is that, instead of draining the greatness from our culture, we increase it.

I believe this dynamic of honor in relationships was actually one of the main things Paul addressed in Second Corinthians 3. He began by drawing this picture for the Corinthians:

> *You are our letter, written in our hearts, known and read by all men; being manifested that you are a letter of Christ, cared for by us, written not with ink but with the Spirit of the living God, not on tablets of stone, but on tablets of human hearts* (2 Corinthians 3:2-3).

He then compared this image with the image of Moses coming down the mountain with his face shining and the tablets of stone in his hand. These two images represent two different covenants. And the shining face of Moses had no glory, Paul says, compared with the glory we possess as "living letters." (I think this is why the Bible is a closed canon. The story can no longer be contained on tablets and paper, for it is now being written on the ever-increasing parchment of human lives through the centuries.) In some ways, the shining face of Moses seems more accessible and therefore more real than the glory we are supposed to be able to see in one another. I personally have never seen someone's face shining so much that I couldn't look at it, and I can tell you that I would remember if I had. But it has certainly happened, and I imagine this kind of manifestation will be seen more as the Church goes *"from glory to glory."* But the point is that Moses never went "from glory to glory." His glory faded, because that glory was only on the surface, only in the visible realm. The greater glory we have is internal and unseen, written on the heart.

This superior glory cannot be simply "seen"; it must be "read" by the one who has learned to read the language of glory. The process of learning to "read" the living letters of one another's hearts is a challenge, but it is central to the process by which we go from glory to glory. Consider again the conclusion to this chapter:

> *But to this day whenever Moses is read, a veil lies over their heart; but whenever a person turns to the Lord, the veil is taken away…But we all, with unveiled face, beholding as in a mirror the glory of the Lord, are being transformed into the same image from glory to glory, just as from the Lord, the Spirit* (2 Corinthians 3:15-16,18).

Under the Old Covenant, a "veil" covers the dimension of the heart, the realm of the Spirit. But when we turn to the Lord, this veil is removed and we gain the capacity to perceive what is unseen, which includes both Christ and those who are seated in Christ. Thus, I propose that when we think of "beholding" the glory of the Lord in the face of Christ, we need to remember that this necessarily involves the discipline of beholding Christ in the faces of one another. Paul went on to say the same just a little later in his letter:

> *Therefore from now on we recognize no one according to the flesh; even though we have known Christ according to the flesh, yet now we know Him in this way no longer* (2 Corinthians 5:16).

We must learn to say of the people we meet what Mother Teresa said of the poor she served: "Each one of them is Jesus in disguise."[3] For as we learn to see Christ reflected in the faces of one another, we begin to use the measure He used in honoring us to honor one another. This creates a flow of life, a flow of grace, which brings what is unseen to the surface in our lives and closes the gap between Earth and Heaven.

My church community understands the basic mission of the Body of Christ to be *"on earth as it is in heaven"* (Matt. 6:10). This is why honor has become one of our core values. We are not just looking to feel good about ourselves. We understand that Heaven comes to Earth when we see glory in one another, call it out, and make room for it to be expressed. We understand that treating people as God sees them is often the key to helping them see themselves as God sees them. This revelation enables them to live as the glorious sons and daughters they truly are in Christ. Ultimately, we believe that this culture of honor will create such a weight of glory, such a flow of life and greatness, that it turns the tide of destruction that dishonor has brought into our society.

So I challenge you to pursue an upgrade in your ability to see and "read" the language of glory written on the hearts of those around you. Pray, as the apostle Paul prayed, that *"the eyes of your heart may be enlightened, so that you will know…what are the riches of the glory of His inheritance in the saints"* (Eph. 1:18). Allow the Holy Spirit to show you any dishonor in your heart and mind, and be quick to repent. Look for low places where you can serve people and lift them up. And seek always to measure people according to the measure of Christ, for it will come back to you, life for life, glory for glory, honor for honor.

Endnotes

1. Blue Letter Bible, "Dictionary and Word Search for *kabowd* (*Strong's 3519*)," Blue Letter Bible 1996-2011, http://www.blueletterbible. org/lang/lexicon/lexicon.cfm?strongs=H3519; accessed January 31, 2011.

2. Blue Letter Bible, "Dictionary and Word Search for *metanoeō* (*Strong's 3340*)," Blue Letter Bible 1996-2011, http://www. blueletterbible.org/lang/lexicon/lexicon.cfm?strongs=G3340; accessed January 31, 2011.

3. "Mother Teresa Quotes," *Catholic Bible 101*, http://www. catholicbible101.com/motherteresaquotes.htm; accessed January 30, 2011.

Chapter 11

SHEKINAH

Then the cloud covered the tent of meeting, and the glory of the Lord filled the tabernacle (Exodus 40:34).

SHEKINAH Glory. I don't know how familiar this phrase is to you, but it is one that I have often heard throughout my Christian life and assumed I basically understood. *Shekinah* often comes up when people are describing the most striking supernatural appearances of the glory of God. The very sound of the word seems to evoke the sense of mystery and awe associated with such appearances. I also assumed it was a biblical word, especially because I had noticed it in the margins of my study Bible (a *Thompson Chain Reference* NASB). But when I began to study *Shekinah*, I was surprised to learn, first, that this word is never actually used in Scripture, and second, that it has a more specific meaning than I had thought.

Certainly, the reality *Shekinah* refers to is clearly expressed in the language of the Bible, though not using that particular word. This is true of many of the words we use to express biblical ideas. You'll never find the words *Trinity* and *incarnation* on the pages of Scripture, for example, though these concepts are directly derived from what is written there. *Shekinah* is one of the oldest of such theological terms. Rabbis commenting during the intertestamental period created the word by taking the Hebrew verb *shakan*, which means "to dwell,"[1] and making it a noun. However, they distinguished it from *mishkan*,[2] the other noun derived from *shakan*, usually translated "tabernacle," for *Shekinah* does not refer to any specific place, person, or building in which the presence of God dwells. Rather, it reveals that the nature of the presence of God is that it "dwells" or "abides." *Shekinah* essentially means, "The dwelling place of Him who dwells." Thus, my study Bible notes "Shekinah glory" in the margins whenever "glory" (the manifest presence of God) and "dwelling" or "abiding" appear together.

God is the God who dwells. This is one of the primary dimensions of His glory, and unless we establish this in our thinking, we will not be prepared to see that glory. When we read the Scriptures, for example, it is possible to come away with the impression that, rather than being the God who dwells, God is more of a visitor to the world He created. Particularly in the Old Testament, vast stretches of time are unaccounted for, where it seems as though manifestations of the presence of God were few and far between. But when we trace *Shekinah* more closely through the Scripture and look for the God who dwells, we discover a beautiful progressive revelation of God's eternal plan to dwell with us.

From The Garden to the Tabernacle

My Bible doesn't have a margin reference in the first few chapters of Genesis, but I suggest the revelation of *Shekinah* begins here with the picture of Adam and Eve, clothed in the glory of God, sharing life with Him in The Garden. In the beginning, God and man dwelt together. We can hardly imagine what that "household" must have been like; all we really know is that when Adam and Eve sinned, they had to leave it. The consequence of the Fall was that the human race became homeless. We ceased to be family members authorized to extend the borders of the home across the earth and became sojourners and aliens forced to seek survival in a hostile environment, barred from our original dwelling in God's glory by cherubim and a flaming sword.

But that was only the beginning of the story. Centuries later, on top of a mountain engulfed in a supernatural cloud, Moses saw those cherubim again when God instructed him to build a replica of His heavenly dwelling. God wanted an outpost among His exiled people, one that would begin to reveal His desire to bring them back to their true home. Accordingly, instead of guarding the entrance to His house, the cherubim stood over the place where God would dwell and interact with them: "*There I will meet with you...above the mercy seat, from between the two cherubim which are upon the ark of the testimony...*" (Exod. 25:22). And though Moses, Aaron, and the high priests after them were the only ones allowed to go before the Ark in the Holy of Holies, all of Israel knew where the *Shekinah* was, for they witnessed two of its primary manifestations, the cloud and the fire, move into the Tabernacle.

The cloud came first, after the Tabernacle was complete:

> *...Thus Moses finished the work. Then the cloud covered the tent of meeting, and the glory of the Lord filled the tabernacle. Moses was not able to enter the tent of meeting because the cloud had settled on [shakan] it, and the glory of the Lord filled the tabernacle* (Exodus 40:33-35).

The fire followed, after Moses had anointed all the priests with blood and oil and made the proper sacrifices:

> *Then Aaron lifted up his hands toward the people and blessed them, and he stepped down after making the sin offering and the burnt offering and the peace offerings. Moses and Aaron went into the tent of meeting. When they came out and blessed the people, the glory of the Lord appeared to all the people. Then fire came out from before the Lord and consumed the burnt offering and the portions of fat on the altar; and when all the people saw it, they shouted and fell on their faces* (Leviticus 9:22-24).

And from then on, the cloud and the fire of the *Shekinah* became the center of Israel, their true home. Whenever it moved, they moved:

> *Throughout all their journeys whenever the cloud was taken up
> from over the tabernacle, the sons of Israel would set out; but if
> the cloud was not taken up, then they did not set out until the
> day when it was taken up. For throughout all their journeys, the
> cloud of the Lord was on the tabernacle by day, and there was
> fire in it by night, in the sight of all the house of Israel* (Exodus
> 40:36-38).

From the Tabernacle to the Temple

An event parallel to the inauguration of the Tabernacle occurred a few
centuries after that, at the dedication of Solomon's Temple. This move from
a tent to a temple was significant for many reasons, but perhaps the most
significant was that God did not initiate it. It was David who first insisted
that the Ark of the Covenant had to be near him in Jerusalem, and then
desired to build a permanent house for it. He ended up entrusting this task
to his son Solomon, but Solomon made sure to announce its true origin at
the dedication ceremony:

> *He said, "Blessed be the Lord, the God of Israel, who spoke
> with His mouth to my father David and has fulfilled it with
> His hand, saying, 'Since the day that I brought My people Israel
> from Egypt, I did not choose a city out of all the tribes of Israel in
> which to build a house that My name might be there, but I chose
> David to be over My people Israel.' Now it was in the heart of
> my father David to build a house for the name of the Lord, the
> God of Israel. But the Lord said to my father David, 'Because
> it was in your heart to build a house for My name, you did well
> that it was in your heart'"* (1 Kings 8:15-18).

David's heart to build a house for the Lord was the most obvious expression of the *"one thing"* he desired—to dwell with the Lord. And it so happened that dwelling with His people was also the thing in God's heart. But

more, what was in God's heart was this mutual desire of man and God to dwell together. This is why God didn't choose a city or a building, but chose a man after His heart, and then fulfilled what was in the man's heart. Though He wouldn't let David build the Temple, He gave him the detailed plans for it just as He had done for Moses (see 1 Chron. 28:19), enabled Solomon to build it (a seven-year project requiring an estimated $18 billion in materials and labor), and ultimately, He moved into it.

Fittingly, the arrival of the *Shekinah* in this new home was accompanied by something that hadn't been present at the Tabernacle of Moses:

> *And it came to pass when the priests came out of the Most Holy Place…and the Levites who were the singers, all those of Asaph and Heman and Jeduthun, with their sons and their brethren, stood at the east end of the altar, clothed in white linen, having cymbals, stringed instruments and harps, and with them one hundred and twenty priests sounding with trumpets—indeed it came to pass, when the trumpeters and singers were as one, to make one sound to be heard in praising and thanking the Lord, and when they lifted up their voice with the trumpets and cymbals and instruments of music, and praised the Lord, saying: "For He is good, for His mercy endures forever," that the house, the house of the Lord, was filled with a cloud, so that the priests could not continue ministering because of the cloud; for the glory of the Lord filled the house of God* (2 Chronicles 5:11-14 NKJV).

At the Tabernacle, the cloud had descended in silence. At the Temple, the cloud descended amidst a glorious concert of His people making *"one sound,"* for this house was a manifestation of the mutual desire of God and man to dwell together. And after the cloud, once again, came the fire, in the sight of the whole nation:

Now when Solomon had finished praying, fire came down from heaven and consumed the burnt offering and the sacrifices, and the glory of the Lord filled the house. The priests could not enter into the house of the Lord because the glory of the Lord filled the Lord's house. All the sons of Israel, seeing the fire come down and the glory of the Lord upon the house, bowed down on the pavement with their faces to the ground, and they worshiped and gave praise to the Lord, saying, "Truly He is good, truly His lovingkindness is everlasting" (2 Chronicles 7:1-3).

The *Shekinah* remained in Solomon's Temple for just over 400 years, a period in which, tragically, Israel carried out a long failure to remain faithful to their covenant with God, resulting in their captivity in Assyria and Babylon. In a dramatic vision he received early in this captivity, the prophet Ezekiel witnessed the departure of the *Shekinah* from the Temple as the Lord brought judgment on the city for their idolatry (see Ezek. 8-10). In a later vision, the Lord showed Ezekiel the detailed plan for rebuilding His house, as well as the return of the *Shekinah* (see Ezek. 40-43). However, the biblical accounts of the rebuilding of the Second Temple do not record the return of the *Shekinah*. "According to the Babylonian Talmud," says the *Jewish Encyclopedia*, "the Second Temple lacked five things which had been in Solomon's Temple, namely, the Ark, the sacred fire, the *Shekinah*, the Holy Spirit, and the Urim and Thummim."[3]

From the Temple to a House of Living Stones

The *Shekinah* did not return to another building because, once again, God had chosen a man instead. This man was called both the Son of David and the Son of God, and it was also in His heart to build a house, but not a house of cedar and gold. He Himself was the house. John wrote:

The Word became flesh, and dwelt among us, and we saw His glory, glory as of the only begotten from the Father, full of grace and truth (John 1:14).

The Greek word translated "dwelt" is *skenoo*, which means "to fix one's tabernacle or tent."[4] It is equivalent to the Hebrew *shakan*. The abiding, glorious presence of God, the *Shekinah*, "tabernacled" among us in the man, Jesus Christ.

Jesus Himself announced that He was the next revelation of *Shekinah*, the dwelling of Him who dwells. He declared that He was greater than the Temple (see Matt. 12:6), prophesied its destruction (see Matt. 24:1-2), and appropriated the term *temple* for Himself:

Jesus answered them, "Destroy this temple, and in three days I will raise it up." The Jews then said, "It took forty-six years to build this temple, and will You raise it up in three days?" But He was speaking of the temple of His body (John 2:19-21).

This statement not only marks the transition from God's dwelling place being a building to it being a Person; it also reveals something about what was to come next in this progressive revelation. As I said, Christ came to build a house. He did not come just to tabernacle among us but to make us part of that tabernacle. The great mystery of the cross is that, by allowing the house of His body to be destroyed, Christ was positioned to rebuild it, and in rebuilding it, to bring all of humanity into the house, to make us His Body. And from this point on in Scripture, the "temple" or "house" of God is always connected to the Body and bodies of believers:

So then you are no longer strangers and aliens, but you are fellow citizens with the saints, and are of God's household, having been built on the foundation of the apostles and prophets, Christ Jesus Himself being the corner stone, in whom the whole building, being fitted together, is growing into a holy temple in the

Lord, in whom you also are being built together into a dwelling of God in the Spirit (Ephesians 2:19-22).

You also, as living stones, are being built up as a spiritual house for a holy priesthood, to offer up spiritual sacrifices acceptable to God through Jesus Christ (1 Peter 2:5).

As He had promised, Christ built this house in three days, when He was crucified and resurrected. But when did the *Shekinah* fill the house? I believe the Gospels and Acts describe a series of events that fulfill the pattern set by the Tabernacle and the Temple. Both times, the cloud first filled the houses, and later fire came and consumed the sacrifices. I suggest that the disciples were first filled when Jesus appeared to them on the day of His resurrection, *"breathed on them and said to them, 'Receive the Holy Spirit'"* (John 20:22). Bible scholars note that this directly parallels the language of Genesis, when God breathed into Adam and he became a living being (see Gen. 2:7). When the "cloud" of His breath filled the disciples, He imparted His Spirit to them and made them a new creation.

Then, Christ instructed the disciples to wait in Jerusalem until they received power—the promised baptism of *"the Holy Spirit and fire"* (Luke 3:16). Obediently, they *"all with one mind…continually* [devoted] *themselves to prayer"* (Acts 1:14), for just as it had been at Solomon's Temple, this posture of united worship prepared the way for the presence of God to come. Meanwhile, as Moses and Solomon had done while Israel was worshiping and waiting on the Lord, Christ was applying a sacrifice. According to Hebrews 9, the sacrifices at the Tabernacle and the Temple accomplished two things: they inaugurated (or in Solomon's case, renewed) Israel's covenant with God, and they cleansed everything in the houses for divine use, for *"all things are cleansed with blood"* (Heb. 9:22). But the houses, sacrifices, and covenant of Moses and Solomon were all lacking in their ability to fully cleanse sin and couldn't have done otherwise, for they were all dealing with copies, not ultimate realities. Christ, on the other hand, brought a sacrifice—the superior sacrifice of His own blood—into the very Holy of Holies in Heaven. This *"one sacrifice for sins for all time"* (Heb. 10:12) finally and fully cleansed us, thus ending the separation between God and man. The curtain in the Temple of Herod was torn at the Crucifixion as a picture of what Christ's sacrifice did in Heaven—it established a *"new and living way which He inaugurated for us through the veil, that is, His flesh"* (Heb. 10:20).

When the blood of this "better sacrifice" had been applied, the cleansing accomplished, the new way opened, the New Covenant inaugurated, and the people prepared in worship, the fire fell:

> *When the day of Pentecost had come, they were all together in one place. And suddenly there came from heaven a noise like a violent rushing wind, and it filled the whole house where they were sitting. And there appeared to them tongues as of fire distributing themselves, and they rested on each one of them. And they were all filled with the Holy Spirit and began to speak with other tongues, as the Spirit was giving them utterance* (Acts 2:1-4).

The Day of Pentecost was the day when the Jews celebrated Moses receiving the Old Covenant on Mount Sinai. When the fire fell on the disciples on that day, it couldn't have been clearer: the old was gone, and the new had come. The *Shekinah* no longer rested on a box, or in a building, or just on one man. Instead, the infilling presence (cloud) and baptism (fire) of the Holy Spirit rested in and upon all believers. We became the dwelling place of Him who dwells.

Carrying the *Shekinah*

So where does this progressive revelation lead us? Well, first, there are two places that it obviously should not lead us. It shouldn't lead us to think that the glory we carry came from us. This, again, is the sin of humanism. Incidentally, painted on the walls of the Library of Congress in Washington,

DC, is a quote from a great saint and one of the ancient fathers of the Church, John Chrysostom. He said, "The true Shekinah is Man." Unfortunately, these words have been co-opted by humanists and used to mean their exact opposite. Instead of acknowledging that we carry a glory that we received from the Glorious One, we have acted as though this glory has always been ours. However, we must not, as many have done, fall into the opposite error by holding back from stepping into the fullness of what we are called to as carriers of the *Shekinah* glory.

The progressive revelation of *Shekinah* is meant to lead us to the simple conclusion that dwelling with God is the whole purpose of our lives. In the words of Christ's command to us, we are to "abide" in Him as He abides in us (see John 15:4). We call this by different names—walking with God, being led by the Spirit, hosting the presence of God—but they all express the central, all-important, lifelong mission of every believer. God took untold centuries and uncounted resources, ultimately paying the unimaginable price of His only Son, in order to painstakingly reveal this mission to us and make it possible. It is the greatest privilege of our lives.

Learning to abide in Christ means allowing the awareness that we are the dwelling of God, the temple of the Holy Spirit, to affect every aspect of how we live. There are many practical aspects to this—far too many to mention here. But I will close by reminding you of several primary ones taught in the New Testament.

The first practical step we must learn to take, and continue to take, is to *draw near* to God:

> *Therefore, brethren, since we have confidence to enter the holy place by the blood of Jesus, by a new and living way which He inaugurated for us through the veil, that is, His flesh, and since we have a great priest over the house of God, let us draw near with a sincere heart in full assurance of faith, having our hearts sprinkled clean from an evil conscience and our bodies washed with pure water* (Hebrews 10:19-22).

Everything in our lives was made to flow out of the center of intimacy with God. Drawing near to Him in prayer and worship, hearing His voice, and communing with Him in His presence is our first responsibility and our greatest joy as carriers of His glory.

Second, in that place of intimacy, Christ told us, we get to ask for things. We've already seen that this is the privilege and expression of sonship; it is also central to our role as carriers of the *Shekinah*. Jesus said, "*If you abide in Me, and My words abide in you, ask whatever you wish, and it will be done for you*" (John 15:7). Those who abide, who walk as the dwelling place of God, ask Him for things.

Third, those who abide steward their bodies, and by extension, all their material resources. As Paul said, "*...your body is a temple of the Holy Spirit who is in you, whom you have from God...you are not your own...you have been bought with a price: therefore glorify God in your body*" (1 Cor. 6:19-20).

Historically, there have been two basic heresies humans have embraced regarding our bodies and our relationship to material reality. One heresy has worshiped our bodies as the source of pleasure and happiness, and the other has called them the source of corruption and sought escape from corporeality. As carriers of the *Shekinah*, we must do neither. Instead, we are called to treat our bodies and everything God has made as holy and consecrated for His use. We abide in Him as we use what He has made for His purposes.

Finally, those who carry the *Shekinah* are called to fellowship with one another. The writer of Hebrews follows the instruction to draw near to God with the consequent instruction to draw near to one another:

> *...let us consider how to stimulate one another to love and good deeds, not forsaking our own assembling together, as is the habit of some, but encouraging one another; and all the more as you see the day drawing near* (Hebrews 10:24-25).

The reality that we are all, collectively, the dwelling place of God forever defines the way we ought to treat one another. Abiding in Christ requires us to honor the glory that dwells in every member of His Body.

Endnotes

1. Blue Letter Bible, "Dictionary and Word Search for *shakan (Strong's 7931),*" Blue Letter Bible 1996-2011, http://www.blueletterbible.org/lang/lexicon/lexicon.cfm?strongs=H7931; accessed January 31, 2011.

2. Blue Letter Bible, "Dictionary and Word Search for *mishkan (Strong's 4908),*" Blue Letter Bible 1996-2011, http://www.blueletterbible.org/lang/lexicon/lexicon.cfm?strongs=H4908; accessed January 31, 2011.

3. *Jewish Encyclopedia.com,* s.v. "The Second Temple," http://www.jewishencyclopedia.com/view.jsp?artid=128&letter=T&search=the second temple; accessed January 30, 2011.

4. Blue Letter Bible, "Dictionary and Word Search for *skēnoō (Strong's 4637),*" Blue Letter Bible 1996-2011, http://www.blueletterbible.org/lang/lexicon/lexicon.cfm?strongs=G4637; accessed January 31, 2011.

Chapter 12

WISDOM: STEWARDING GLORY

And He has filled him with the Spirit of God, in wisdom, in understanding and in knowledge and in all craftsmanship (Exodus 35:31).

W ISDOM Is a word often consigned to the arena of the intellect, which itself has been reduced to the mere possession of information. This is an obvious mistake. I have known a lot of people who had loads of information but who have not necessarily been wise! However, I have also noticed that many of those who have a better understanding of wisdom have not sufficiently recognized the relationship between wisdom and glory, which is established from the first mention of wisdom (Hebrew: *chokmah*[1]) in the Bible:

> *You shall make holy garments for Aaron your brother, for glory and for beauty. You shall speak to all the skillful persons whom I have endowed with the spirit of wisdom, that they make Aaron's garments to consecrate him, that he may minister as priest to Me* (Exodus 28:2-3).

In order for His priests' garments to be glorious, God needed those who made them to have wisdom. More specifically, He needed them to have three things, which in total comprised their wisdom. First, He needed them to be *skillful*. The Hebrew word here literally means "wise-hearted."[2] This indicates that the physical ability by which these artisans wove cloth and worked with precious metals and stones was itself a measure of wisdom, an area of practical knowledge over which they had mastery. Second, they needed *the spirit of wisdom*. This anointing enhanced their natural ability and knowledge and made them supernatural. And finally, they needed *a vision of divine purpose*. It was not until Moses spoke with them and explained the "pattern" of heavenly things he had received on the mountain that their natural and supernatural wisdom became fully active. It was the combination of these three elements that enabled these artisans to take raw materials and use them to realize Moses' vision of these brand-new garments assigned to divine purpose and glory.

These components need to inform and define our understanding of wisdom. Knowledge and skill alone do not comprise wisdom, nor even do supernatural knowledge and skill. True wisdom always involves the partnership of God and man working together to fulfill divine purpose. This relational, collaborative nature of wisdom is clearly seen in Proverbs, the central book of wisdom in the Bible. There Wisdom is depicted as a woman who calls anyone who will listen to come and take counsel with her (see Prov. 1, 8, and 9). Moreover, Wisdom calls herself the *"master craftsman"* or architect who collaborated with God when He created the universe (see Prov. 8:30 NKJV).

As we have explored throughout this book, not only the Tabernacle, but everything created by God was designed to express the heavenly pattern of His glory—His nature, attributes, and character. Wisdom knows this pattern and wishes to speak of it to us so that we, like the Tabernacle artisans, have a vision of divine purpose by which to interact with all that God has made. For, as those made in the image of the Creator, we have a unique role in His creation as sub-creators; we are all artisans, commissioned to enter into an eternal partnership with Wisdom in order to bring creation into the fullness of its glory.

Stewardship is a good biblical word for this commission. It has become a somewhat outdated term in today's economy, but historically, a steward was one appointed to manage the affairs of another's household or estate. The landlord entrusted a steward with the responsibility of making sure that everything he owned was being used properly according to his priorities. In the case of God's household, He appointed an entire race—His own family members, in fact—as His stewards when He commissioned us to be fruitful, multiply, fill, subdue, and take dominion in the earth (see Gen. 1:28).

Of course, each one of us is assigned to manage only a small part of Heaven's affairs on the earth. But our success in stewarding that part requires us to understand how our responsibilities derive from the ultimate purposes of the Master for His household, purposes defined by the pattern of His glory. These include His plans to fill the earth with the knowledge of His glory, to have the Gospel of His Kingdom preached to all people, to make disciples of all nations, to bring all the kingdoms of the earth into His Kingdom, and to make all things new (see Hab. 2:14; Matt. 24:14; Matt. 28:19; Rev. 11:15; Rev. 21:5). In short, He plans to make Earth like Heaven (see Matt. 6:10), and everything we are individually called to do as stewards is part of fulfilling that plan.

True wisdom, I propose, is the skill of *stewarding the glory of God*. Developing this skill requires first that we grow in understanding the relationship between our individual callings and the priorities of our heavenly household. Second, it requires that we learn to use the resources we have been given in order to fulfill these callings. If "stewardship" has become dry and outdated in the Church, it is because we have come under the delusion of Western materialism and thought that we've only been given material resources to steward. We have forgotten that our job is not merely to maintain the earth but to make the earth like Heaven.

For this we have been given both material resources and *"riches in glory"* (Phil. 4:19), the supernatural resources of Heaven. Using these together is never boring—at least, I don't imagine the Tabernacle artisans were bored when they discovered their natural talents had been upgraded by the Holy Spirit in order to turn natural resources into items of exquisite, never-before-seen beauty and glory. I also don't imagine Jesus Christ was bored as He healed the sick, raised the dead, multiplied food, turned water to wine, and otherwise repeatedly demonstrated how effective it is to steward natural resources together with the supernatural resources of Heaven.

In order to be wise stewards, then, we must know our Father's business and how to carry it out using what He has entrusted to us. But the final and most important element in wisdom, in stewarding glory, is faithfulness. Paul said, *"Moreover it is required in stewards that one be found faithful"* (1 Cor. 4:2 NKJV). The center of Jesus' wisdom was not His incredible knowledge of the business of Heaven, nor His wonderful skill in using Heaven's resources, but His unflagging faithfulness to do the Father's business. It was by His faithfulness that Jesus never fell from wisdom as so many others have done.

Take Solomon and lucifer, for example. Both of them received astonishing gifts from God. Their "skill sets" were off the charts, as were the levels of revelation in which they walked. These, of course, were given in order for them to achieve their divine purposes. Both lucifer and Solomon were appointed as worship leaders. Lucifer was made to partner with the angels of Heaven as they enjoyed His presence. Similarly, Solomon was set apart to build a house of worship in Israel and establish a national culture upon the worship of God. Yet they both left the path of wisdom in the same way. They did not stop worshiping. They kept using the gifts and abilities they had received. They just began to direct that worship elsewhere—in lucifer's case, toward himself, and in Solomon's case, toward other gods. As stewards, they were unfaithful to their Master's business, abandoning divine purpose and using His glory for their own ends.

It is easy to be drawn to and impressed by people to whom God has given great talents, abilities, knowledge, wealth, and anointing, and who seem, for all we can tell, to be using all of those things and performing well in life. But when we compare the performance of Jesus to the performance of Solomon and lucifer, we learn the really impressive thing—the choice to loyally and faithfully take every gift before the Giver and devote its use to His purposes. This is the heart of wisdom, of stewarding glory, for this is the only way that the glory we have been given will remain our own. The moment we use our glory for an agenda other than God's, that glory ceases to be ours, for we fall short of it.

Christ's faithful stewardship of glory is our standard and our invitation. Even better, as Isaiah prophesied, He is our *"Wonderful Counselor"* (Isa. 9:6), Wisdom Himself, our partner in stewardship. We can be sure that He will faithfully train us to walk in wisdom as He did.

The Glory of Tension

In His life and ministry, Christ modeled that our stewardship of glory is carried out on the frontier—the frontier between Heaven and Earth, between time and eternity, between what is and what ought to be. Our commission here is to extend the borders of the family estate until everything expresses the glory and purpose for which it was created. And we do this as the Tabernacle artisans did, by taking the raw materials of our lives and the world around us and crafting them into glorious things of worship.

This life on the frontier is one of great tension and conflict. We are living in two realities, and there is resistance between them. The *skill* of wisdom grows as we learn to negotiate this tension, and one of the first steps is realizing that we need tension. I know that for most of us, tension speaks of anxiety and stress, which are proven to be destructive physically, emotionally, and mentally. However, it is equally true that without healthy tension in our lives, we would die. Most of the basic functions of our physical bodies require tension. Our muscles are all arranged in pairs, which work together by creating tension. When we breathe, our lungs extract oxygen from the air through semipermeable membranes, which rely on the tension between differing concentrations on either side, thus forcing the exchange of gases. Likewise, mental health is found in tension. I well remember a lecture given while I was training to become a psychiatric nurse. Of all the lectures I heard, it probably made the most sense to me, and it still does. The central concept was that mental health is the ability to live in the tension of all the conflicting thoughts and experiences that life throws at us while maintaining our ability to be responsible for our actions.

Given the nature of our bodies and minds, it should not surprise us that tension is necessary for spiritual health and growth. At a recent sad, yet glory-filled, memorial service for a courageous young revivalist, Bill Johnson reminded the Bethel family of a tension the apostle Paul called us to walk in: "*Rejoice with those who rejoice, and weep with those who weep*" (Rom. 12:15). If you personally are not rejoicing, then joining in with those who are requires you to step into the tension between your circumstances and theirs, which can be uncomfortable. Likewise, anyone who has tried to comfort the grieving knows the tension involved in helping another shoulder a burden of sorrow. Bill explained so simply, yet so eloquently, that weeping with the bereaved and rejoicing with the joyful, even though our lives may be far removed from theirs at that time, develops in us the heart of Jesus, who Himself weeps and rejoices with us in our circumstances. The one who fully identified Himself with us imparts His life to us as we identify with one another.

Jesus blessed another kind of tension necessary for spiritual health: "*Blessed are those who hunger and thirst for righteousness, for they shall be satisfied*" (Matt. 5:6). The more we learn of Christ, our standard of righteousness, the more we recognize the distance between who we were and who we are becoming. Many believers have struggled with discouragement when they see how they fall short, thinking that the goal is unattainable. But few of us struggle with discouragement when we get hungry or thirsty. We get up and go find something to eat or drink! In fact, we'd be concerned if we didn't get hungry—loss of appetite is usually a sign that we are not all right.

Like our appetite for food and drink, the tension created by our need for His righteousness is a positive thing, meant to drive us to pursue what God has made fully available to us.

Faith is another tension, in fact, the central tension, that we must learn to negotiate wisely for our spiritual growth. Abraham, the father of faith, left a civilized city and spent the rest of his life living in a tent, but his success in God's eyes was not measured by how far he went from that human city, but by how close he came to the city *"whose builder and maker is God"* (Heb. 11:10 NKJV). He lived in the tension between the visible status quo and the wild, supernatural journey to which an invisible God called him, and because he did, he received the first installment of the blessing that would restore spiritual life to the human race—righteousness: *"Abraham believed God, and it was credited to him as righteousness"* (Rom. 4:3). As Paul explains at the end of this chapter, the words *"it was credited to him"* were *"written not for him alone, but also for us, to whom God will credit righteousness—for us who believe in him who raised Jesus our Lord from the dead"* (Rom. 4:23-24 NIV).

We all receive righteousness by stepping into the tension of Abraham's faith and journeying as he did toward our heavenly home.

The tension of faith is also the tension between promise and fulfillment, and I have often observed how vital wisdom is in negotiating this tension. Living as I do in a prophetic environment, I know well how exciting the atmosphere created by the constant declaration of promises can be. People come alive with passion and vision when their dreams and destiny are so often being called out and affirmed. However, I have also seen that the tension of believing in and walking toward the fulfillment of God's promises usually pushes one's hope and faith to the limit. People have told me that they wished the tension created by the prophecies they've received would just go away. They have said they would rather not receive any more prophetic words about a particular promise because it only heightens the uncomfortable contradiction between the promise and their circumstances.

But wisdom teaches us that if God really means to make all things new in and through us, we ought to expect that His promises will be very different than our circumstances. More, according to Peter, God's promises are actually part of His glory, and when He gives them to us, He is giving us something to steward. As we learn to steward the promises of God, He brings out His divine nature in us, which prepares us to steward their fulfillment (see 2 Pet. 1:3-4).

The story of the four lepers in Second Kings 7 is a wonderful parable for handling the tension created by promises. The circumstances of the four lepers were desperate. Not only were they infected by an incurable disease; they were living between a city in famine and an encamped enemy army. The famine in the city was so dire that women were boiling their children and eating them. Donkey heads and doves' dung were selling for a small fortune. (I have no idea, and frankly don't want to have one, of what you would do with a donkey's head.) But when the king called upon Elisha, the man of God, for guidance, Elisha's prophecy that everything would turn around in a day's time put them in the tension between what they could see and the promise.

For the lepers, the difference between their experience and the words of the prophecy couldn't have been greater. And yet the tension created by that contradiction became a source of energy for them to take action. They realized, "We can sit here and die, we can go into the city and die, or we can get up and do something." When they acted on the tension instead of giving in to it, they not only saw the fulfillment of God's promise; they became God's partners in that fulfillment! God did His part by defeating their enemies, but they were the ones who plundered the enemy's camp.

If you are living in circumstances that completely contradict your promises, I want to remind you that you are being positioned to plunder the enemy's camp. God has defeated your enemy and regained all that has been lost and stolen from you. But by His promises, He has delegated you, His steward, to come and get it. Your faithfulness to trust His words before they come to pass will prepare you to be faithful with them when they do. Through faithfulness, the heart of wisdom, you can remain confident that the tension created by God's promises is never intended to overwhelm, crush, or disappoint you, but is rather His tool of training to bring out His divine nature in you and equip you to lay hold of the riches in glory assigned to the fulfillment of your divine purpose.

Wisdom also helps us harness the tension between what we know and what we don't know, to live with mystery. *The Cloud of Unknowing*, a brilliant book written by unknown authors in the 14th century, lays out a simple guideline. It says to take the things in life that we do not know the answers to or understand and place them in the cloud of unknowing to one side of our view of God, so that they do not impede our view of Him. This requires us to hold what we know of God in tension with what we don't know, but if we handle this tension wisely, it will actually strengthen our confidence in what we do know and drive us to know Him more. We will also learn, I've found, that the words *"I don't know"* are some of the most powerful and freeing words we can say.

Of course, we also find mystery and tension in what we do know. Anyone who has found a truth has usually noticed that it consists of two or more truths held in tension. And because God is the source of truth, we find that these conflicting truths are held together in His nature. How does He, at one and the same time, hear the cry of a victim of a sex offense and yet hear the repentance of the perpetrator? And how is it that He takes broken men and women like us, victims and perpetrators alike, and uses us to achieve His purposes? These are some of the deepest mysteries we come up against in God, but the more we accept them as the pattern of His wisdom and endeavor to imitate that pattern in treating people as God treats them, the more we are crafted into those who can carry this tremendous love everywhere we go. We carry the message that He died for the victim and the perpetrator, has made us all His family, and invites all of us, no matter our background, to take our rightful places as His glorious sons and daughters, kings and priests. This is why the Church, the Bride of Christ, is the only organization on the planet that is able to embrace the full spectrum of all people and find their hidden glory.

Barnabas, the great encourager, is an example of one who embraced the tension in God's love. It led him to see the transformation in a former terrorist and bring him before the apostles. It would have been easy and obvious—even what many would have called wise—to polarize Saul the murderer as a threat. But we know now that doing so could have robbed the world of the glory revealed in the 19 letters that the converted Saul wrote. Barnabas prepared the way for God to put the full transformational power of His love on display through a man, the self-named "chief of sinners," who had fully experienced the depth, height, and breadth of the Gospel and become its chief teacher and missionary.

There are many other aspects to the tension we experience living on the frontier of Heaven and Earth. My goal in this section has simply been to show you how we, as stewards of glory, can approach this tension not as an obstacle to divine purpose, but as the very means of achieving it. The very wisdom of the cross teaches us that Christ, the faithful steward of glory, has taken the tension and resistance created by our sin and made it serve divine purpose as the opportunity for His grace to "much more abound" (see Rom. 5:20). This is why the Bible isn't shy about recording the full range of man's weaknesses and failures, even of the heroes of our faith, in its account of redemption. Its message to every generation is that God loves and uses men and women just like us, not because we are perfect, but in order to perfect us.

The Glory of Overcoming

The corollary to the glory in tension is the glory in overcoming. In order to produce health and growth, tension, whether physical, mental, or spiritual, cannot be static but must work within a flow of tension and release. On the spiritual level, we grow and mature as we endure and then overcome various tests of our faithfulness in stewarding glory. Each test we pass qualifies us for a promotion, an increase of responsibility, where we will be tested again. I realize that *test*, like *tension*, is a word most of us don't like very much. But without a battle, there can be no victory. And without victory, there can be no dominion. The process of testing, overcoming, and promotion is the way we take increasing dominion as we've been commissioned to do.

The suffix "dom" in wisdom indicates that it is a "domain" or "dominion," a sphere of judgment or authority. Luke tells us that Christ increased in this dominion throughout His life: *"And Jesus kept increasing in wisdom and stature, and in favor with God and men"* (Luke 2:52). It may seem strange that the Son of God had to grow in wisdom. But He did so because He had come as the "last Adam" to succeed where the human race had failed as stewards and restore our stewardship to us. At every stage, Christ's faithful stewardship qualified Him to receive an increase in the domain of His wisdom, culminating in His final promotion, when God *"highly exalted Him"* (Phil. 2:9) and He received keys—the keys to death and Hades and the key of the house of David (see Rev. 1:18; Isa. 22:22).

Keys are symbols of authority because there is no authority without *access*. I learned this well in my first two careers. When I began my first career as a student nurse at the London Hospital in Whitechapel, England, I remember being very aware, now wearing my new uniform, that I had access to walk through doors I previously would have passed by. These doors were simply marked, "Staff Only." Most of them were unlocked, and there would have been nothing to stop me from walking through them before. But I hadn't, quite simply because I knew that I didn't have permission or authority to walk through those doors. When I eventually left nursing to become a prison officer and then a senior prison manager, this process continued, though during my first weeks of training at the prison, I had to work without having been issued my keys. That was a humbling experience. I do not recommend being a non-criminal in prison without keys! As I was promoted to higher degrees of authority in prison, I received keys that gave me access to more and more doors. Ultimately, as the in-charge governor, I had a master key that gave me unlimited access.

Christ has gained the master keys to the universe and has unlimited access to all things. But even before He received those keys, He promised to give that access to us:

> *I will give you the keys of the kingdom of heaven; and whatever you bind on earth shall have been bound in heaven, and whatever you loose on earth shall have been loosed in heaven* (Matthew 16:19).

As His fellow stewards, Christ wants us to share His authority to access Heaven and bring it to Earth. It is true that to share in this authority, we each must undertake the journey of testing, overcoming, and promotion that He took, but because He has already taken it, He is able to help us at every stage of the journey. However, one of the primary ways He helps us is by having us help one another. He calls us not only to imitate the pattern of His stewardship by overcoming, but also by using our victories and increased authority to help others overcome.

In January 2008, I was diagnosed with prostate cancer. In the spring of that year, I ended up undergoing surgery for its treatment, and I am daily thankful for a successful outcome. After my surgery, however, I collapsed, and for a variety of other reasons, I had an extremely bad time in the hospital. The whole senior management team of Bethel Church came to visit and pray for me at lunchtime on Easter Sunday. I quipped to them that even Jesus went to hell on Easter—but He came back with keys! I wanted my keys!

A few months after my successful treatment, I had occasion to visit a store to discuss an item that was being made for me. On entering, the owner recognized me and asked where I had been, hoping there had not been anything serious that had kept me away. I replied that I had a radical prostatectomy for cancer. Without a moment's hesitation, this man, with whom I had only had conversations about my purchase, opened up and said that he had the same operation ten years earlier. In a matter of seconds, I entered into quite an intimate conversation with him. He told me of his disappointments and regrets following the surgery. I was able to ask him a couple of questions, look him in the eye, say that he had made the right decision, and explain the reasons why. With quiet reassurance, I was able to begin to lift a load from this man's shoulders that he had carried for ten years.

Through this encounter, I saw that I had indeed received my keys. I had been given increased access to this man's life—not, I hasten to add, for a reason I would have volunteered to have, but access nevertheless. But here was the significant thing—on the human level, the only thing necessary for that man to give me that access was that I had shared his experience. And if that were all that had happened, it wouldn't have meant much more than exchanging sympathies. More had happened, however—where he had only survived his test, I had overcome mine and gained wisdom. This positioned me not only to walk through that door of access, but once through it, to impart that wisdom to him and give him the benefit of my victory.

I suspect that we all regularly encounter doors that we have authority to enter because of the wisdom we have gained through overcoming in places of tension and trial. Whether you are a mother who has reared a child through the terrible twos, or one who has experienced the journey of a son being sent to war and coming home safely, increased wisdom is available to you with which you can help someone else negotiate those narrow paths of life. However, I think many of us are not using the access we've been given as much as we might do, perhaps because we don't always feel like powerful overcomers. We're still more aware of the times we've failed our tests than we are of the victory Christ has already won for us. But Christ reminds us, "...*take courage; I have overcome the world*" (John 16:33).

No matter where we are on our journey of overcoming areas of weakness and failure, we can be sure that if we stay with Him, we will share in His victory and see Him redeem every failure for an increase in our wisdom. Instead of disqualifying us, our areas of failure and weakness will become the very places where we have authority. When I meet someone saved from a life of drug addiction I am not surprised to see that he or she helps others with addictions; in fact, it is the sign that he or she has truly overcome and received authority in that area. The ones who have overcome have authority to help others overcome.

This is the very principle at work in letters of the apostle Paul. I don't think there exists a believer who has not been profoundly blessed and strengthened by Paul's words:

> *For I am convinced that neither death, nor life, nor angels, nor principalities, nor things present, nor things to come, nor powers, nor height, nor depth, nor any other created thing, will be able to separate us from the love of God, which is in Christ Jesus our Lord* (Romans 8:38-39).

Where did Paul gain the authority to declare this with such emphasis? He gained it through the many tests he endured, described in Second Corinthians 11:23-28—he was imprisoned, in danger of death, beaten, shipwrecked; he suffered sleepless nights, experienced hunger, and weathered almost every imaginable kind of trauma. Paul survived every possible threat to his life and found that none of it could separate *him* from the love of God. Paul wasn't a writer of dry theology. He lived a biography in which he overcame in the most extreme circumstances, and when he declared the testimony of the wisdom he had gained through overcoming, he gave us the truths that became our theology, and have helped generation after generation of believers to overcome.

Revelation 12:11 says, "*They overcame...by the blood of the Lamb and by the word of their testimony...*" (NKJV). The blood of the Lamb is the victory we receive. Our testimony is the victory we have to give away. As I lay in the hospital recovering from surgery, I overcame by standing on the victory Jesus had won through His blood. But when I left the hospital, I had something else—the word of my testimony of overcoming—and I have determined to use this word to overcome again, and help others to overcome. I encourage you to do the same with your testimonies. We mustn't waste our victories. Each one has given us a key to access Heaven and bring it to Earth in our lives and in the lives of others. Wise stewards don't simply walk around with keys. Wherever they have access, they are about their Master's business.

Endnotes

1. Blue Letter Bible, "Dictionary and Word Search for *chokmah (Strong's 2451)*," Blue Letter Bible 1996-2011, http://www.blueletterbible.org/lang/lexicon/lexicon.cfm?strongs=H2451; accessed January 31, 2011.

2. Ibid.

Chapter 13

GLORY THROUGH GATES OF PEARL

And the twelve gates were twelve pearls… (Revelation 21:21).

YOU'VE Probably heard the phrase, "You can't take it with you." It's usually used as an excuse for being reckless with money. But you can take something with you. Heaven is designed for you to take your glory with you. In Revelation, it says that *"the kings of the earth,"* which reasonably includes all of us who have become *"kings and priests"* (Rev. 5:10 NKJV), will carry our glory into Heaven through 12 gates made of 12 pearls:

> *And the twelve gates were twelve pearls; each one of the gates was a single pearl.…and the kings of the earth will bring their glory into it* (Revelation 21:21a, 24b).

This passage happens to be the key verse in my favorite of my father's sermons. I decided to include this sermon in this book, not only because it presents a wonderful insight into glory that has shaped my own perspective, but because, together with the experiences of my sons James and Luke, it makes this a story lived out by three generations of Manwarings, an expression of our family DNA and legacy. Two of these generations have never met, but I who bridge the gap between them see clearly how both my sons manifest their grandfather's DNA to an extraordinary extent. My sons live as if they had known my dad. I know that James' passion for music and his ability to conduct and lead bands, choirs, orchestras, and most recently, an opera, have his grandfather on his feet cheering in the great cloud of witnesses. Luke's love of soccer reminds me of sitting with my dad, watching England win the 1966 World Cup on our newly acquired black-and-white television set. Dad's love of sport and photography lives on in Luke. And we all share the most precious legacy Dad left to us: his faith.

After my father died in 1973, I found an old notebook of his stored in our attic. It was in an old metal chest and could easily have been thrown away among the other seemingly worthless items he left there—pencils, notebooks, and some old engineering tools. Fortunately, I did not throw it away, and it is one of my favorite and most cherished possessions. Together with my family and photographs, it is the item that I would most want to retrieve in the event of a disaster. The notebook contains handwritten sermons, as well as the details of when and where those messages were preached. It is an insight into my father that I never had when he was alive, a constant reminder of his faith and my family DNA.

My father preached the following message in June 1957 in Chadwell Heath, London, England, at a Congregational Church where my uncle Billy, my dad's brother, was the minister. He was the man who collected me from school on the day Dad died, and the man who led me in prayer beside my dead father's bedside. My mother was in the congregation, pregnant with me, when my father gave this message.

The 12 Gates Are 12 Pearls

There is in the 21st chapter of Revelation a marvelous description by John of the place Jesus went to prepare, describing Heaven in all its glory. He says that the walls are of jasper, the city of pure gold, and the foundations are garnished with all manner of precious stones. And the 12 gates are 12 pearls. Much has been written about the meaning of these precious jewels, and I certainly cannot give you a theological exposition of their meaning, but I want to reflect for a few minutes on the gates of that city and to consider the meaning of the entrance to the new Jerusalem, for as John says, it is by a pearl that we enter. The 12 gates are 12 pearls. It is an agreed fact that pearls are the product of pain. Sometimes the pain is caused by a worm or boring parasite, or the shell of the oyster gets chipped or pierced and a speck of sand forces its way inside. Immediately, all the resources of the tiny organism rush to the spot where the breach has been made. On the foreign body, the unsuspected healing powers of the little creature are marshaled at the point of peril. In that hour of mortal danger, and only in that hour, the oyster exudes a precious secretion in order to close the breach and save its life. Powers that otherwise would forever have remained dormant are called out in this emergency. The foreign body is covered and the wound is healed, by a pearl.

No other gem has such a fascinating history. It is a symbol of stress, a tiny creature's struggle to save its life. We don't normally associate pearls with pain. Pearls are for the ballroom. Pearls are for the hours of entertainment and relaxation amongst the chandeliers. How attractive they look. Pearls share in the sparkle and gaiety of those who try to forget for a while that life has its sober side. But pearls are not made that way. Their history is much in contrast to their use. They are not the product of pleasure; they are the product of pain. If there had been no wound in the oyster shell, there would be no pearl.

Our stress and our struggle in life may be divine agencies leading us to that celestial city. What did Sara Adams write in that great hymn? "So by my woes, to be nearer my God to thee."

The world's sufferers are in the forefront of the world's philanthropists. They lead to better things. It was the tragic death of a young doctor stricken by heart failure that turned the attention of Sir James Mackenzie to cardiology. He was inspired by pain to enter those studies, which resulted in his great work on the diseases of the heart. The loss of the liner Titanic led to the establishment of the Atlantic Ice Patrol. There is a famous and beautiful suspension bridge by the old town of Conway in North Wales. It is over 100 years old. Why was it built? Was the ferry outdated? Did they want to travel faster? No, that was not the motivation for the building. It was that on Christmas Day, 1806, the mail boat capsized in crossing the River Conway and 13 people were drowned. It was then, and only then, that the authorities began to talk about a bridge. Lighthouses are built for similar reasons. Roads are widened after tragedies. It would be true to say that if no one suffers, no one cares.

I think we shall get nearer the theme if we notice the power of suffering in the lives of people that suffer themselves. The Gentiles were evangelized by an apostle with a thorn in his side, and you cannot separate his sufferings from his success. It was the blinded Milton who sang so divinely in *Paradise Lost*. It was the imprisoned Bunyan who wrote that great masterpiece, *Pilgrim's Progress*, and it was the deafened Beethoven who wrote the immortal 9th symphony. Who will dare say that their distresses had nothing to do with their triumphs?

Some time ago there was unveiled in the ward of a London Hospital a plaque to the memory of Mandombi, the late chief of Nigeria, Africa. The story leading up to the erection of the plaque is a remarkable instance of self-sacrifice by a member of the so-called backward races on behalf of the rest of the world. Over 30 years ago, Mandombi became a Christian under the guidance of the late Dr. Grattan Guinness and shortly afterward was stricken with the terrible disease of tropical countries, sleeping sickness. With the sad fate upon him, Mandombi conceived the idea of making the rest of his life one great sacrifice for mankind. He communicated to Dr. Guinness his desire that he might be made the subject of experiment for the benefit of other sufferers, and he was brought to England and installed in a London hospital under the care of several eminent doctors. This was the first case of its kind in England and was admitted solely in the interests of finding a cure. Part of the research required the examination of his blood every four hours for two months! This research was rewarded by the eventual discovery of the cause of the disease. It was not possible to save Mandombi's life, but through his self-devotion and sacrifice, literally millions of lives have been saved around the world. Through the terrible disease of an old black chief so soon after he became a Christian, Jesus, having entered his soul, allowed the creation of a great pearl.

Human nature is frail. We shrink from disappointment and disabilities, sickness, and failing strength. But they have a ministry to those that dwell in Christ and in whom Christ dwells. They are golden opportunities to make something worthy. Some people complain that they have endless trouble and others have none. That just isn't true. Life taken as a whole visits all. Some people react differently. Some make heavy going of it, and some shake it off. The same trouble that makes one person sour will make another person sweet. That devastating blow that makes one man a cynic will be used by another as a stepping stone to a nobler life.

Have you a grudge against life and God? Can you learn a lesson and turn your pains and disappointments into pearls?

A line of verse in one of our daily newspapers caught my eye the other day: "God and the Doctors we alike adore, but only when in danger not before. The danger over, both are alike requited, God is forgotten and the Doctor slighted." That verse was written by John Owen around about the year 1660, and frankly human nature is no different today.

It is our need that drives us to God. I suggest that we pray most when we feel the need most—when sickness, worry, depression, or the dark mysteriousness of life has us in its grips. The dangers we dread the most drive us to expand ourselves in spirit.

I want to suggest that pain and disappointments are paths to progress, the possibility of making a pearl just like the oyster, the means by which the dormant side of our character, the nobler side, is drawn out. Have we always got to wait until disturbing influences enter our life before we start creating the gem? And if there is no wound, can there be no pearl? God forbid that despair and despondency must overtake us before we find the gate to the celestial city! There is no life in which disappointment, the hard, and the unpleasant do not play their part. No life is exempt from trial, and every trial is an opportunity to start making a pearl!

Let us bring the matter down to commonplace, if some insist that they are an exception to the rule, that nothing of any magnitude has ever upset the smooth running of their lives. Even being the subject of third- or fourth-hand gossip about you, which has been embroidered on the journey from tongue to tongue, can leave you angry and upset. The unkind, unjust, and untrue can fester and create resentment in your heart. But here is an opportunity to make a pearl. We can call episodes like that wounds of the spirit. Can you then staunch its bleeding by forgiving the originator of the slander? Can you begin the process of healing by prayer for them? Jesus Christ is called the pearl of great price. There can be no wonder at that when the King of Calvary's hill dying on the cross, surrounded by His murderers, says, "Father forgive them, they know not what they do."

Or perhaps it was by disappointment that your opportunity came. Don't let disappointments make you sour or bitter or cynical. Do you know the story of Henry Martyn and his great disappointment? He had given his all to God, his gift of languages, and God called him to the mission field, and then he fell in love. Few men are faced with a more difficult choice than this, and Martyn's mind was tormented with indecision. His work or his love? After much deliberation, he chose the work to which God had called him, and then followed his farewells, the embarkation at Portsmouth, England, although he had an unexpected stop as an impulsive last visit to Lydia, his love, holding on to half-tantalizing hopes that she might agree to join him.

Martyn buried himself in his work and books. Life had no interest but his work. He said that he wished to have his whole soul swallowed up in the will of God, but very soon sickness took him and he died at Toact in Asia Minor, a young man without so much as a single Englishman near him to hear his last words. He died at 31 years of age, but his work had been accomplished, the New Testament translated into Hindustani, Persian, and Arabic. Here was a man whose life, though full of disappointment, was made into a pearl. Can we—I know that I haven't made all that I could have— but can we take even the small irritations of life and make pearls? The smallest pearls are called seedlings; the largest, which can be the size of a walnut, are called paragons. May the pearl of great price and the Holy Spirit so work in you that you produce paragons.

It is clear to me that my dad had a revelation of how we enter Heaven. The revelation I'm not sure he had, but which I have been invited to walk in, is that Heaven is not just the reality that lies beyond physical death for the believer but is in fact the reality we are called to access and live from in this life. I believe the pearls we make as we submit pain and irritation to the foot of the cross, where the Holy Spirit covers them in resurrection life, will adorn us for the marriage supper of the Lamb and into eternity. But I also believe that these pearls open gates by which we enter ever deeper into that reality here and now. Not only that, the reality we learn to live in is the reality we will get to invite others to experience. In the last chapter, I said that our victories give us keys of authority that open doors for us in the lives of others. But another way to describe it is that the experiences that form pearls in our lives enable us to become pearlescent gateways through which others can walk. I don't know about you, but this gives me even greater motivation to embrace the pearl-making opportunities that come before me. They are invitations to know glory and to bring others into the knowledge of glory, as the apostle Paul described:

Blessed be the God and Father of our Lord Jesus Christ, the Father of mercies and God of all comfort, who comforts us in all our affliction so that we will be able to comfort those who are in any affliction with the comfort with which we ourselves are comforted by God (2 Corinthians 1:3-4).

This message is a part of my DNA, and it continues to shape my understanding of the design and purpose of Heaven. Heaven is designed for glory! I recently read the famous poem, *The Divine Comedy*, by Dante, in which there is the line describing the gate of hell. Above the gate is a banner, declaring, "Abandon hope, all ye who enter here."[1] The entrance of Heaven declares the complete opposite, for there we pass through gates created by the suffering of One for all and come to the place where we meet our deepest hopes at last. And as we produce pearls in our own lives, we become doorways of hope that lead others to glory.

Dad, thanks for your great message. It got me through the toughest times and now into the best of times. It even prepared me to be a part of Bethel staff, where Pastor Bill Johnson has taught that while God does not always deal the hand, He wins with every hand He's dealt. You taught me, by this message, that pearls are the product of pain submitted to the cross of Jesus—pain not sent by Him but crafted by the Great Comforter, the Holy Spirit (after whom surely the inside lining of the oyster shell, the mother of pearl, is named). That process produces the beauty that is the pearl. It's why Bethel is my tribe, and you would have loved it, too!

Endnote

1. Dante Alighieri, *The Divine Comedy*, "Inferno," cto. 3, l. 9, (1321).

Chapter 14

THE GLORY OF FREEDOM, COVENANT, AND JUSTICE

You cannot train a man for freedom under conditions of captivity.

—Sir Alex Paterson

FOR 11 of my 19 years in prison management, I served in young offender institutions. In each of these institutions, part of the regime was that all of the prisoners were allowed temporary releases and home leaves where they could be tested in varying degrees of freedom as they prepared for release. These allowances, especially those in which the young person failed to return or committed another crime, were often misunderstood and criticized by the public and media. Sometimes, of course, there were errors. But there were reasons for this policy that made it worth its risks. It was based on a principle established by Sir Alex Paterson, one of the founders of the young offenders' prison system, quoted above: "You cannot train a man for freedom under conditions of captivity."

Paterson understood something that generation after generation has struggled to understand, once they have grasped that we are living in a fallen world. They see on the one hand that human beings naturally desire freedom, and on the other that we continually prove that we are not capable of handling it very well. How is it that an omnipotent God who claims to be good has allowed us to make such a mess of things? Why did He trust us with freedom? I think the film *Bruce Almighty* tackled these questions in a hilarious but profound way. In the film, God endows the frustrated Bruce with all His power, with the one prohibition that he is not allowed to interfere with free will. Bruce discovers that, though he can walk on water, answer prayers, and pull all sorts of supernatural pranks, the one thing he wants, the love of Grace, his girlfriend, is the one thing he can't take by force. Love must be freely given, or it is not love. In the end, Bruce learns that he can only invite Grace to love him by using his own freedom to love her sacrificially and unconditionally.

Love is exactly what God, who is love, wants most from His children—wants it so much, in fact, that He was willing to give us freedom and risk the consequences of our misusing it. But He only did so because He knew that no consequence, even death, was beyond His redemption. He knew that, in fact, our failures would only afford Him the opportunity to put His great sacrificial, unconditional love into motion and so invite us to reciprocate by learning to love as He loves. The great lengths to which He has gone to free us from captivity to sin tell us that God believes we are capable of learning to handle freedom. It is this godly belief that humans can and need to be trusted with freedom that has guided leaders like Sir Alex Paterson and has motivated every great move toward freedom throughout history.

Today, however, in our Western society largely founded upon a value for freedom, many people speak of freedom as though it were merely the lack of restraints or obstacles. But any thinking person ought to see that some restraints are good and some are bad, so mere removal cannot be true freedom. Unseating a tyrant, abolishing slavery, or cancelling an oppressive law are steps toward freedom, but so are establishing just laws and leaders. Real freedom does not consist in the lack of restraints but in the individual's power to choose, and to choose what is good.

The progressive revelation in Scripture of how God is training the human race to walk in freedom clearly supports this. The difference between the Old Covenant and the New Covenant is not that the first restrained our behavior and the second did not. Both introduced a law that restrained, but the first was an external law and the second was internal. The Old Covenant restrained us externally because, before Christ, we lacked the spiritual power to choose goodness, being separated from God by sin. But now that we have been reconciled to God, made alive in Christ, and given His Spirit of power, love, and self-control (see 2 Tim. 1:7 ESV), we have that capability. Now that this power to choose (self-control) has been restored to us, we find that its nature is necessarily two-sided. Saying yes to one thing means saying no to everything else. Choosing what is good necessarily means resisting what is evil. Thus, every free choice defines a boundary, a limitation, and a constraint.

Freedom has limits because it has a design and purpose. The secret to freedom is that when we use it according to its design, its limits do not diminish our freedom but cause it to flourish. Freedom was designed for love and nothing else. I've said freedom is the power to choose what is good, but the choice to do good is always the choice to love. As the lawyer correctly replied to Jesus, the entire moral teaching of the law and prophets, the volumes and volumes of instruction on how to choose good and avoid evil, boils down to this: "'*You shall love the Lord your God with all your heart, with all your soul, with all your strength, and with all your mind,' and 'your neighbor as yourself'*" (Luke 10:27 NKJV).

The rendering of Galatians 5:13-15 in *The Message* clearly expresses the truth that freedom was designed for love:

> *It is absolutely clear that God has called you to a free life. Just make sure that you don't use this freedom as an excuse to do whatever you want to do and destroy your freedom. Rather, use your freedom to serve one another in love; that's how freedom grows. For everything we know about God's Word is summed up in a single sentence: Love others as you love yourself. That's*

> *an act of true freedom. If you bite and ravage each other, watch out—in no time at all you will be annihilating each other, and where will your precious freedom be then?*

The glory of freedom, then, derives solely from the glory of love, which means that we cannot have freedom by seeking it as an end in itself. It is only by learning to love that we learn to be free and come to know the glory of freedom. Perhaps you've heard the story from Bob Jones about his heavenly encounter where he saw each person being asked a single question before they entered into glory. The question was simply, "Did you learn to love?" This really sums up the whole point of history. God has made His choice— He chose us first, in all our imperfections, and loves us. In doing so, He invites us to express the same aspect of His character: "...*choose...today whom you will serve...*" (Joshua 24:15).

There is a learning process to this choice, as the question, "Did you learn to love?" indicates. We will have to learn to give up lesser gods in order to discover that only He can satisfy the deepest longings of our hearts. We will have to choose to trust that He knows best how we ought to choose and learn to align our wills with His. But if we do, we will find that these are actually all acts of freedom. Christ, whose will was perfectly submitted to His Father's, was the freest human being ever to walk the planet—His power of self-control, His power to choose love in every circumstance, was consummate. He is the standard for all members of the eternal royal family. Heaven is populated with lovers, not conscripts, all of whom have chosen freely to be there, with no doubt of motive or sincerity, no hidden agendas. The rewards of Heaven belong solely to those who embrace the lifelong journey of learning to love, and in doing so, have become fully and gloriously free.

Of course, from the outside, love can look like anything but freedom. Lovers make what seem to be continual sacrifices for one another. Parents make sacrifices for their children. And before we understand it, the sacrifice of the cross can seem too terrible a price for God to pay for us. The risks and costs of love can seem to lay obligations and demands on you that would diminish your freedom. But it does not feel like that on the inside of real love. It is true that those who choose love risk disappointment, rejection, and abuse of their affections. It is true that they may be required to pay a great price for love; in fact, they must prepare themselves to give everything. But for those who truly love, the risks and costs of love are not deterrents but attractions, for they serve to reveal the preciousness of the beloved, the worthiness of the choice. Neither do lovers perceive these risks and costs as limits on their freedom. In fact, they know that it will be precisely in the moments when their love cannot be repaid or returned that the freedom of their choice will be most clearly revealed. This is the pattern of love in the Gospel. The price God paid to love us did not rob Him of His freedom; it revealed its magnitude, for there is no greater act of freedom than the choice of a perfect God to love imperfect humanity. In loving us, God has shown us that the things to which true lovers say no simply cannot compare with the great prize to which they have said yes. There is no price, only reward.

Learning to love as God loves will require us to become as free as we can possibly be, to reach the full potential of our willpower, and this process confronts all of us with the degree to which the relational dynamics we grew up with have either equipped us or failed to equip us to handle freedom. A child who has been loved well at home learns more or less to value and respect his or her own personhood and that of others and is empowered both to make choices and to honor others' choices. Unfortunately, however, many children are not loved well, and I have often observed how difficult it is for those who have been abused or neglected to make healthy choices and create boundaries in their lives. Lacking value for themselves, they struggle to find anything to which they really want to say yes, and struggle to say no when other things or people control them. Sadly, when this prison is all you have known, freedom appears very frightening. A person with a history of abuse can find even something as simple as ordering from a menu a daunting challenge! People cycle through these destructive patterns in relationships and life because they simply don't know how to break free.

The glorious message of the cross is that there is no person so broken, bound, or bankrupt that God cannot restore to freedom and empower to love. The remarkable story of the man of the Gadarenes reveals that even a person possessed by thousands of demons still possesses his God-given free choice to hand himself over to God. And the Bible shows that as soon as the man did so, Jesus began to restore his personhood to him, clothing his body and speaking to him as a free man, finally entrusting him with the great honor and responsibility of bearing witness to Him (see Mark 5:1-20). This is what God does for us. God made us for love and freedom—made us for Himself—and when we make the smallest choice to trust Him with our lives, He begins to bring to life all of the places that have been damaged through abuse or neglect, restoring our dignity and desires and teaching us to walk as free men and women, bound by nothing but love.

The Glory of Covenant

The Old Testament reveals a pattern in the way that God chooses us, and therefore, in the way He invites us to choose Him in return. Beginning with Noah and followed by Abraham and his descendants, the people of Israel, God called out His chosen people by inviting them into a relationship established and defined by a covenant.

A covenant has two primary elements—a statement detailing the commitments of the relationship, and a promise to faithfully honor those commitments. In the case of God's covenant with us, the first element, the commitments He calls us to walk in, are actually revelations of how we were made to live. We've already seen how He created us in His image for relationship with Him and one another, and His Covenants, Old and New together, show us the specific design for that relationship. The Bible also shows that everything God created thrives and prospers when it functions as He designed and breaks down when it does not. In our case, our fulfilling or not fulfilling God's design for relationship is literally a matter of life and death. But part of that design, again, is that we have a free choice in the matter. This is why Moses declared the following to Israel after reviewing the guidelines of God's covenant:

> *See, I have set before you today life and prosperity, and death and adversity; in that I command you today to love the Lord your God, to walk in His ways and to keep His commandments and His statutes and His judgments, that you may live and multiply, and that the Lord your God may bless you in the land where you are entering to possess it. But if your heart turns away and you will not obey, but are drawn away and worship other gods and serve them, I declare to you today that you shall surely perish. You will not prolong your days in the land where you are crossing the Jordan to enter and possess it. I call heaven and earth to witness against you today, that I have set before you life and death, the blessing and the curse. So choose life in order that you may live, you and your descendants, by loving the Lord your God, by obeying His voice, and by holding fast to Him; for this is your life and the length of your days, that you may live in the land which the Lord swore to your fathers, to Abraham, Isaac, and Jacob, to give them* (Deuteronomy 30:15-20).

"Choose life...by loving the Lord your God." We either choose to bring our lives into harmony with God as we walk before Him in relationship, or we choose to violate that relationship. The choice to love or not to love is the choice between life and death. This serious, black-and-white nature of covenant is why the second element of covenant—the promise-making—is accompanied by certain ceremonies, which initially can be strange or even gruesome to us. The word *covenant* comes from a root that means "to create by cutting." When God made His initial covenant with Abraham, Abraham cut animals in half and the presence of God walked between them, an act that essentially said, "You can do to me what you did to these animals if I break my covenant promises" (see Gen. 15). Later, God added another "cutting" to this covenant—the rite of circumcision that was to mark every male

in Abraham's line. When the Old Covenant was given at Sinai, there was more cutting—God cut out the tablets of the testimony and cut His laws into them with His finger, and many animals were cut and sacrificed. In every case, these "cuts" were irreversible. These physical realities were to remind the people that their covenant with God had created something that could not be changed without serious consequences—life and death consequences.

Covenant creates "one flesh." Scripturally, of course, this phrase belongs specifically to marriage. But as we learn from the apostle Paul, marriage is a reflection or derivative of the larger covenant reality between Christ and the Church. Paul said, *"For we are members of His body, of His flesh and of His bones"* (Eph. 5:30 NKJV), and *"...So we, who are many, are one body in Christ, and individually members one of another"* (Rom. 12:5). This is the fundamental truth of our being as covenant people, and it needs to define our thinking and behavior if we are going to live in relationship as we were designed. This is the reality behind our call to honor, to perceive the face of Christ in one another so that we learn to love one another as we love Christ, and to love Christ as we love one another.

Being *"members one of another"* actually leads us to take the Golden Rule further or at least to understand more fully how it works. In covenant, we not only know that we ought to love one another as we love ourselves; we know that it is *by loving one another that we love ourselves.* This is what Paul said was true about marriage:

> So husbands ought also to love their own wives as their own bodies. He who loves his own wife loves himself; for no one ever hated his own flesh, but nourishes and cherishes it, just as Christ also does the church, because we are members of His body (Ephesians 5:28-30).

I personally have discovered the glory of this mystery, that by loving my wife I love myself, and that we choose life as we honor the covenant we've made with God and one another. The greatest decision of my life, apart from salvation, was to agree with my wife's desire to leave our home and careers in England and move to Redding, California. Though initially this wasn't my desire or plan, loving her was my desire and plan. With this priority in my heart, I sought the right decision, only to discover that, as she began to see the plan that God had for her life, I saw God's hand more clearly in mine. God had been preparing both of us for this because He had made our two lives one. Our journey to Bethel Church in Redding constantly reveals to me God's love and plan for our lives. He prepared me long before the decision—not just to make the decision to come, but also to be able to step into the opportunities that decision opened up to me. In a way, I was like Moses, raised in Pharaoh's house for a mountaintop experience many years later, and many miles away!

Covenant expands our understanding of the Great Commandment as well as the Golden Rule. We are to love God with all our heart, mind, soul, and body, and as Jesus explained, this means doing what He tells us to do: *"If you love Me, you will keep My commandments"* (John 14:15). But if we take the Ten Commandments as representative of the whole, at least 70 percent of God's commandments are about loving one another. God's covenant guidelines indicate that, just as we love ourselves by loving one another, so do we love Him by loving one another. This is why Christ taught that whatever we do to the least of His brothers, we do to Him (see Matt. 25:41-45). He was not speaking figuratively when He said this; He was describing the nature of covenant reality.

Christ was also talking about this covenant reality when He said:

> *The glory which You have given Me I have given to them, that they may be one, just as We are one; I in them and You in Me, that they may be perfected in unity, so that the world may know that You sent Me, and loved them, even as You have loved Me* (John 17:22-23).

When we were *"united with Him in the likeness of His death"* (Rom. 6:5), God cut a covenant with us in the body of His Son and made us "one flesh," imparting His substance to us. This adds yet another dimension to the previously mentioned verses in Peter. We partake of His divine nature through His *"precious and magnificent promises"* (2 Pet. 1:4) because they are covenant promises, agreements we share because we have become one with God Himself.

The Glory of Justice

God designed us to live in this incredible network, this living tapestry of relationships, where life and prosperity flow as we love Him and one another. However, we can only appreciate the beauty and glory of this tapestry through God's progressive covenant revelation through history, and that progression did not begin with us experiencing life as He designed it. It began with God showing us, through His covenant with Israel, just how far we were from that design, and how we had arrived there. It began with the revelation of sin. The Law God gave to Moses was not an arbitrary set of rules God set up to exert His power; it was the revelation of His standard for relationship so that we could see what sin really is—the violation of relationship. Only when we recognized that we were made for relationship and we had chosen to cut ourselves off from life by rejecting our own purpose and design could we recognize and receive God's provision to heal the consequences of sin and restore relationship. This was the whole purpose of the Old Covenant—as Paul said, *"...the law was our tutor to bring us to Christ..."* (Gal. 3:24 NKJV).

But even from the beginning of God's lesson plan for teaching us His relational standard and the nature of sin, we find that He was promising to restore us back to life in relationship with Him as we were designed. And we find this promise right in the center of the declaration He made to Moses on the mountain when He showed him His glory. As God passed Moses in the cleft of the rock, He announced that He:

> *...forgives iniquity, transgression and sin; yet He will by no means leave the guilty unpunished, visiting the iniquity of fathers on the children and on the grandchildren to the third and the fourth generations* (Exodus 34:7).

The Hebrew word translated *forgive* literally means "to bear," or "to carry off."[1] And the phrase *by no means* is an emphatic negative that creates, in effect, an oath or a promise. Essentially, God promised Moses that He would bear the weight of our sin and make sure that the payment for it was taken care of. He would take it upon Himself, in fact, to ensure that there would be One down the line of the generations of "children" and "children's children" who would finally pay the debt of Adam.

This is the justice of God, and it is part of His glory. He not only reveals His standard and design for relationships to us and calls us to choose it; He also takes personal responsibility to uphold that standard and restore us to it when we violate it. This is how far His covenant love extends: because He loves us as He loves Himself, He actually is willing and able to fulfill our end of the covenant when we fail to fulfill it ourselves, even to the point of taking on the consequences of our failure. This is the unfathomable formula stated by Paul:

> *He made Him who knew no sin to be sin on our behalf, so that we might become the righteousness of God in Him* (2 Corinthians 5:21).

It is a great mystery that a glorious, perfect God is able to *"be sin."* It is a great mystery that the Son of God who is entirely one with His Father was yet able to be cut off from Him on the cross, to take on our violated relationship. But that is the glory of His justice—promised to Moses and fulfilled by Christ.

This understanding of the glory of justice sheds important light on the psalmist's statement: *"Righteousness and justice are the foundation of Your throne…"* (Ps. 89:14). Many people view righteousness as compliance with a set of rules given by a controlling God and justice as what happens to you when you don't comply with the rules. But biblically, righteousness is living in alignment with God's standard in relationships, and justice brings restoration when that standard is violated. Just as we *"justify"* text on a word processer by lining up with a standard in relationship to the right, left, or center of the page, God justifies us by aligning us with His relational standard. I believe this one verse alone, if understood relationally, would radically change the culture of the world in which we live. Two millennia after the cross, the world still needs to learn that *the purpose of justice is the restoration of relationships.*

Having had the privilege of working in Her Majesty's Prison System for England and Wales, I'm very familiar with what most people in the United States and United Kingdom associate with the term *justice,* and I'm also aware that it's very easy to mistakenly project that association back onto biblical justice. But they are very different things. At least, Jeremiah 9:24 says that God delights in justice. If God delights in justice, then I have to say that it must be a radically different experience of justice than I had working in the criminal justice system.

That said, however, there have been thinkers and leaders, like Sir Alex Paterson, who have had a vision for applying a more biblical vision of justice in the prison system. Some of them developed a "justice model," which I learned about early on in my career. The historical background for the justice model is this: until 200 years ago, prison was a place to hold someone awaiting trial. After the trial, the punishment that followed was a fine, flogging, or death. Today in England, the death penalty has been eliminated since 1965, and only very recently has there been a life sentence that actually meant life. Thus, for most offenders, a trial is followed by a prison sentence and eventually a return to free society, a transition that can be just as difficult as going to prison in the first place. In the justice model, the purpose of the prison sentence is not punishment but rehabilitation to prepare the prisoners for a successful return home. In many ways, it resonates with the biblical goal of restoring relationships. However, with this goal, the justice system can leave many victims unsatisfied. Many of them turn to the legal system to make offenders pay for their offenses. Situations like this have contributed to justice losing place to the demands of the law. Even our language has changed to reflect this. Police officers used to be called peace officers. Now we talk of law enforcement.

As believers, we cannot look to human institutions to define justice; we must view human institutions through the lens of biblical justice and seek to apply it with or without institutional support. My wife once showed me a way to apply biblical justice in my job in a situation where there was simply nothing in the system to guide me. Early in my career as a prison manager, I served at Maidstone Prison in Kent, England. This was in the days before pay phones were available for prisoners to use, and they had to request to make a phone call. One Sunday morning, a young man in his twenties asked permission to make a phone call that afternoon, as it was his young son's birthday. This request was outside of the general rules for phone calls— phone calls were for emergencies and legal matters. I lived near enough to the prison to go home and have my Sunday lunch with my wife. Unusually, we discussed that application and I asked her advice. Her reply was simple and profound. She pointed out that it was not his son who had committed a crime. What had he done to deserve being deprived of talking to his dad on his birthday? It was a perspective that I was to apply on many occasions after that, a perspective based on a child's birthright to have a relationship with his or her parents. Living in relationship with a father is righteous living, and in this case, justice, albeit in part, restored that standard.

We find one of the best examples of biblical justice in the story of Solomon and the two mothers (see 1 Kings 3). Two women were brought to him with one living and one dead baby, arguing over to whom the living baby belonged. What a task Solomon faced. This story predates DNA testing by millennia. The two women with their claims, and with the absence of witnesses and scientific evidence, could probably have argued their case for a very long time. But Solomon's understanding of God's design for relationships gave him the knowledge that a mother will fight for her child's life regardless of personal cost. This is instinctive to earthly mothers, but it also shows us an aspect of God, who would pay the great price of His Son for His children. And so, Solomon issued the outrageous yet profoundly wise instruction to divide the baby into two pieces. There were gasps, I am sure, by all in attendance. Maybe there was a pause, though I suspect the response was immediate for the real mother, as that is the nature of instinct. "Let her have the baby," she declared. And there Solomon had all he needed to know: the one who gave birth would rather lose custody than see her offspring die. It was pure genius because it was the heart of God. He willingly lost custody of His Son for a season in order that His children might not die.

When the truth came out, Solomon was left to pronounce judgment, and that he did, *in favor* of the one who declared, "Let her have him." He judged for her and for the baby. He judged according to the purpose of justice: the restoration of relationships. There was no punishment meted out, no further mention of the conspirator who sought to steal a baby after the tragic loss of her own. The story ends by informing us that, as a result of this judgment, Solomon was regarded as the greatest judge of his day.

Like Solomon, the Judge of all the earth will judge *for us*—in our favor. We all too often consign the word *judgment* to a finding of guilt, and we think finding guilt is a judge's primary job. But when God sent judges to His people in the Book of Judges, they were sent to deliver: *"Then the Lord raised up judges who delivered them from the hands of those who plundered them"* (Judges 2:16). The Judge of Heaven is the great Deliverer, and His ultimate justice will be fulfilled when everything He died to deliver and restore is made manifest. This is the true significance of Judgment Day in Revelation. There will be punishment on that day, but that is not the main event. The glory of Judgment Day is that it is the day when Jesus finally gets what He paid for, His Bride and His restored family of brothers and sisters!

We also mistakenly use *"judgment"* to describe destructive effects on the planet that are more properly the consequences of incorrect alignment—the curse that came upon the earth through sin (see Gen. 3:17-18). But through the cross, God has broken that curse and made provision for all misalignments to be corrected—justified. The restoration of relationship He purchased for us includes the restoration of our relationship with the planet. Thus, the real "judgment" of God will be seen, not when the earth manifests destruction, but when it manifests harmony and health under the care of the sons and daughters of God.

God has commissioned us as the carriers of His justice to the world. Remember, the mere declaration of His justice, in the declaration of His goodness, caused Moses' face to shine. Now, through the glory we know "*in the face of Christ*," we not only shine with the declaration of His justice; we are the very manifestation of that justice. Every time we forgive, make and keep promises, bring life and healing to people's bodies and souls, and otherwise mend and strengthen relationships, we apply the justice of the cross. Just imagine a society of fully restored relationships—that is the end-time agenda. No man has put it better than Dr. Martin Luther King in the less-quoted closing words of his glorious speech, *I Have a Dream*:

> I have a dream that one day the state of Alabama, whose governor's lips are presently dripping with the words of interposition and nullification, will be transformed into a situation where little black boys and black girls will be able to join hands with little white boys and white girls and walk together as sisters and brothers.[2]

Taken from their context in divine relationships, freedom and justice have lost much of their definition and power, even as they remain commonly accepted as some of our most-esteemed cultural values. It is my dream to see an entire generation of covenant lovers, glorious sons and daughters, arise in the true freedom of Christ's love and carry His justice of restoration to the world. I can't imagine anything more glorious.

Endnotes

1. Blue Letter Bible, "Dictionary and Word Search for *nasa' (Strong's 5375)*," Blue Letter Bible 1996-2011, http://www.blueletterbible. org/lang/lexicon/lexicon.cfm?Strongs=H5375&t=KJV; accessed January 31, 2011.

2. "I Have a Dream," "Martin Luther King Speeches," Martin Luther King Online, http://www.mlkonline.net/dream.html; accessed January 31, 2011.

Chapter 15

GLORY AND GOVERNMENT

There will be no end to the increase of His government or of peace...
(Isaiah 9:7).

AT Bethel Church, we pursue the mandate expressed in the prayer Jesus taught us to pray: *"Your kingdom come. Your will be done on earth as it is in heaven"* (Matt. 6:10). This prayer reveals God's clear intention that anything that isn't in Heaven shouldn't be on Earth, and anything that is in Heaven should be on Earth. It's really very simple: everything bad shouldn't be here and everything good should be! Anyone who encounters Bethel, whether through books, podcasts, our schools of ministry, or conferences, knows that we passionately pursue Heaven on Earth in the area of healing. We believe miracles ought to be an expected part of daily life, and in particular, we are pursuing a specific goal in the area of healing: a cancer-free city. There is no cancer in Heaven and neither should there be on Earth—or any other disease, for that matter!

But of course, the mandate *"on earth as it is in heaven"* extends far beyond our physical health and has implications for every area of life and society. Along with a cancer-free zone, our ultimate vision is to see the reality of the Kingdom of God transform every aspect of our city, from schools to businesses, arts, media, families, and government. Because of my personal passion and gift in administration, this last arena, government, is one I have especially been pressing into, asking what the government of Heaven is like and how it can be expressed on Earth.

The Greek word translated *government* in First Corinthians 12:28 is *kybernesis*,[1] which is derived from a word that means "to steer." A possible rendering of *kybernesis* is "steering toward the vision." There is no government without a vision, and more, the vision must define the ways in which that vision is pursued, that is, the system of government. As John Adams wisely said in his "Thoughts on Government," "We ought to consider what is the end of government, before we determine which is the best form."[2] So what is the vision of Heaven's government?

Some time ago, while I was developing the government structure for our network of churches, Bill Johnson made a simple statement. He said that the best model for understanding Heaven's government is family. This has stayed with me until the present day and become a phrase that I chew on regularly. Many of the reasons for understanding Heaven's government as family we've already seen in this book. We saw that God said, *"Let Us make man in Our image"* (Gen. 1:26), revealing God Himself to be a family who began all things by creating a family. We have also seen that He commissioned the human family to be fruitful, multiply, and fill the earth, and then to take dominion of it (see Gen. 1:28). In other words, Heaven's government authorized the human family to imitate God by *creating family* and by *ruling as family*. These two things lie at the core of the vision of Heaven's government.

We also know that only two chapters after God laid out the design and commission of the human family, we became estranged from Him through the Fall and came under a curse that blighted our family relationships and the earth we were made to govern. But what we must realize is that our exile in the kingdom of darkness never revoked Heaven's vision. It simply set the stage for Heaven to fulfill it in an even more glorious way. Into the midst of

God's shattered image of humanity, the Son of God came with *"the govern-ment...on His shoulders"* (Isa. 9:6). Contrary to the expectation of the men who followed Him, He did not come to overthrow their human oppressors and set up His government in Jerusalem. Instead, through the revolution of His perfect obedience and sacrificial death, He overthrew the *"god of this world"* (2 Cor. 4:4) and *"sat down at the right hand of the throne of God"* (Heb. 12:2).

Mysteriously, when He ascended to the throne, He did not do so alone, but rose "[leading] *captive a host of captives"* who were *"seated...with Him in the heavenly places..."* (Eph. 4:8; 2:6). And by the same death and resurrec-tion through which Christ restored us to a ruling position, He also restored us as family. Christ became the *"firstborn among many brethren"* (Rom. 8:29), the founder of a new human race, a new family of glorious sons and daugh-ters. But this restoration to our original commission of making family and ruling as family changed the nature of and position by which we do both. Now we enter by the new birth into a family that rules from Heaven itself and transcends all class, generation, gender, and race. We become disciples of our King and Elder Brother in preparation to rule and reign with Him, and through our witness, we draw others into the same reality and process.

Those of us who embrace this new birth embrace with it the hidden wis-dom of Heaven's government revealed by the cross. This wisdom is built on the truths we discussed in the previous chapter, that God has set us free in order to love one another, and that it is in loving one another that we are free. This is why a relational God entrusted us from the beginning with author-ity to govern—specifically, to govern ourselves by submitting to the law of love—and why His Son paid the highest price to restore that authority to us, not to stage a political coup. Even today in nations that have inherited the value of freedom and self-government, this wisdom appears as foolishness to those who only know financial, military, or political human power. But Heaven's government works from the inside out. Christ said, *"...the kingdom of God is within you"* (Luke 17:21 NKJV). The only real change in the world comes from individual men and women who make the willing choice to have a revolution of repentance and establish the government of Christ in their own hearts and lives.

Apostolic Government and the Gift of Government

It is noteworthy to me that the move of God in which Bethel is participating combines two very strong and clear themes: inner healing and apostolic government. At first glance, these may seem disparate pursuits. But they are connected by a biblical principle, the principle that we can only establish the Kingdom around us to the degree that the Kingdom is established within us. We can only take dominion in the name of the King to the degree that we are under His dominion. The inner healing journey is the journey of the Kingdom being increasingly expressed in our bodies, souls, habits, and character, while apostolic government establishes the Kingdom in the Body of Christ and the world. To put this in relational terms, inner healing is the process of restoration in our individual relationships with God and others, for all areas of brokenness in which we need healing can be traced to relational wounds and disappointments. As we are restored, we become carriers of the relational glory required in an apostolic government.

Apostolic government is the system, the *administration suitable to the fullness of the times,*" by which Christ steers His Body toward His vision, "*... the summing up of all things in* [Him], *things in the heavens and things on the earth...*" (Eph. 1:10). It is also called the fivefold ministry, but in both passages where Paul describes the governmental appointments in the Church, Ephesians 4 and First Corinthians 12, the apostle is first on the list, so we generally shorten it to apostolic government. I won't describe each appointment in Paul's lists in detail, but I will point out that they clearly indicate church leadership is not designed as a one-man show. It is designed as a team—as a family, in fact. Paul called himself a father (see 1 Cor. 4:15), and in Ephesians 4, he described the role of Christ's government as a parenting role. The result of its administration is that the Body becomes "*a mature man*" with the "*measure of the stature which belongs to the fullness of Christ,*" and *"are no longer...children"* (Eph. 4:12-14). Unless those with fivefold appointments understand that they are first fathers and mothers in Christ's family, they won't be able to fulfill that responsibility effectively.

We will look at two particular aspects of fathering in Heaven's government in a moment, but before we do, I want to discuss briefly one gift of Christ in Paul's list in First Corinthians 12 that is not listed in Ephesians 4, but which is clearly part of Christ's government. It is the gift of government or administration. In my experience, "administration" and "government" are frequently misunderstood in the Church. I have met many people who received a prophetic word that they were administrative, interpreted it to mean clerical, and rejected the prophecy or at least delayed it. I have also met with people who received a word regarding government and assumed it was speaking of the political arena. Of course, in many cases that association is correct. But these terms must be put in their proper biblical context in order to be understood:

> And God has appointed in the church, first apostles, second prophets, third teachers, then miracles, then gifts of healings, helps, administrations, various kinds of tongues (1 Corinthians 12:28).

Notice that this list is both a list of gifts and a list of appointments, and *"administrations"* (government) is among the gifts. I consider it a requirement that every leader in the Church possess the gift of government in some measure, in addition to the other gifts associated with his or her appointment, because it is this gift that enables all of the others to work together to build up the whole Body. The gift of government helps leaders to discern the differences between the various gifts and appointments as well as the way they were designed to function in relationship to each other, and enables them to carry out their roles in a way that honors these relationships.

There are three main elements that the gift of government brings together in leading the Body of Christ—the relational element, the creative co-laboring element, and the organizational element. The relational comes first, for again, this is the foundational design of Heaven's government. The highest priority of government is creating an environment where healthy relationships grow, and the success of government is measured by the quality of relationships it fosters. The gift of government helps leaders to correct strife, competition, division, and other relational misalignments and establish strong relational bonds.

Second, because Heaven's government is relational, it is co-laboring and creative. Fruitfulness always flows out of intimacy. When relationships thrive, collaboration thrives—not only because people who get along like to do things together, but also because they desire to share a common vision and journey of life. The gift of government enables the Church to develop this common vision and creatively move toward it.

Finally, precisely because it is creative, Heaven's government is organized with systems and structures to facilitate creativity and collaboration. I have often heard people say things like, "We don't plan. We are led by the Spirit." I do recognize that many plans have wrongly replaced the leadership of the Holy Spirit, which is our priority. However, making plans and being led by the Spirit are not mutually exclusive. The Holy Spirit is the supreme Planner and Organizer. We must never use the Holy Spirit as an excuse for not organizing; to do so is to deny the organizational genius of the Holy Trinity. To discover this genius, of course, we must surrender our inferior, limited versions of planning and organizing, but not in order to stop planning and organizing. Rather, we must ask Him to train us and equip us to use His gift of government.

Now, if we look at the world's models of government, we will find measures of success in promoting healthy relationships, creativity and collaboration in a shared vision, and effective strategies for planning and organization. Much of this success is very impressive. But we must understand that they only seem impressive because we have not yet seen fully what will happen when an entire community is united in relationship and co-laboring with

God in a Holy-Spirit-led plan to fulfill Heaven's vision. Unfortunately, many Christian leaders have prevented people from pursuing their relational, creative, and organizational potential in God by looking to the world's models and systems and trying to imitate them instead of looking to Heaven for our inspiration. Earth's models of government inevitably slide toward management, maintenance, and politics, which are particularly deadly to a Church called to live as pioneers on the borders of Heaven and Earth. Leaders in the Church must courageously seek only to reflect the glory of Heaven's government with the unshakable conviction that Christ's Body is not called to follow the world. Instead, we are to be the examples, the educators, the ones whose lives and examples point to God. We are the ones through whom the world will be transformed until *"… The kingdom of this world has become the kingdom of our Lord and of His Christ…"* (Rev. 11:15).

Fathering Generations

Pursuing the vision and priorities of Heaven's government, which are eternal, necessarily reshapes our relationship with everything in time and space. Instead of aligning ourselves with nations, classes, races, or genders, or with a particular decade or era, we begin to align ourselves with the eternal purposes and family of God. We begin to become aware that we are connected to our human family and the Body of Christ around the planet and throughout the centuries both before and after us. We begin to think generationally, and we begin to think globally.

It is the responsibility of those God has appointed as governors in His Church, the mothers and fathers, to train the Body of Christ to think generationally and globally, and especially to think with the core value of honor. Bill Johnson once asked a provocative question: "How far can you go with a government of honor?" As I have considered this question, I have seen that honor is the key that brings an eternal government into time and space.

In the earlier chapter on honor, we saw that life flows through honor and that the Body of Christ goes from glory to glory as we learn to honor (recognize the glory) in one another. We need to realize that from Heaven's eternal perspective, this truth also applies to honoring past and future generations. As Bill Johnson often points out, every living generation is like a runner in a relay race. All of us hold a position of being a middle generation, responsible to receive the baton of glory from the previous generation, run with it as hard and fast as we can, and then hand it off to the next. This is another picture of how we go from glory to glory.

As I have shared, I am particularly aware of holding the position as the linking generation in my own family because my sons never met my father. Before I reconnected with him through my imagination as I have described, though I never willfully dishonored my father, I was kept from seeing and acknowledging much of the glory he had to pass on to me because of areas in my thinking that had not been corrected by Heaven's perspective. When my mind was renewed in regard to my father, I came into agreement with the heavenly reality of our relationship and honored it properly, which is why life began to flow through that "artery" again—life that I can now pass on to my sons.

The history of Elijah and Elisha teaches us much about how to receive a spiritual inheritance and what happens when an inheritance is not passed on. Elisha was passionate in honoring his spiritual father and did his utmost to make sure that he received Elijah's baton when he left the planet. As soon as he received that baton, he began to run with it (see 2 Kings 2). But when Elisha died, his spiritual sons failed to repeat his example and his baton, his prophetic and miracle anointing, went to the grave with him:

> Elisha died, and they buried him. Now the bands of the Moabites would invade the land in the spring of the year. And as they were burying a man, behold, they saw a marauding band; and they cast the man into the grave of Elisha. And when the man touched the bones of Elisha he revived and stood up on his feet (2 Kings 13:20-21).

When a spiritual inheritance is not passed on, it is not destroyed, but future generations are robbed of its benefit. However, I am convinced that God protects the inheritance of His saints and will not allow mantles of anointing or wells of revival to be forgotten and unused forever. The very fact that many in the Body of Christ have begun to think generationally and are visiting the graves of saints and the sites of revival to pray for us to receive those inheritances is a sign of this. I also think there are inheritances that have been found but are being misused, which God will take care to restore to their divine purpose and glory. Moses declared, *"...the things revealed belong to us and to our sons forever"* (Deut. 29:29).

Every increase in knowledge, every discovery or breakthrough, is properly the inheritance of the family of God and is purposed to enable us to fulfill our commission as governors of the planet. Since the establishment of Christianity, we have witnessed at least four major breakthroughs that have set the stage for global revival—the shift from a flat to a round earth, the invention of the printing press, the advent of electronic communications (television, radio, telephone), and the Internet. These breakthroughs have been used to serve many purposes contrary to God's, but it is the responsibility of His glorious sons and daughters to appropriate these inheritances and seek Holy-Spirit-led strategies for using them to "steer toward the vision" of Heaven's relational government. It has become one of my desires, as I oversee a global network of churches, to leave this life, not with a plugged well or an anointing left in a grave, but with a flowing river that goes far into the future. In order to do this, I understand that I must study the past in order to regain lost inheritances. Whenever we study the past—whenever we look at any human life, for that matter—we will find both the glory of God and areas that fall short of that glory. The core value of honor is the only thing that enables us to avoid letting a person's shortfalls obscure our view of his or her glory. The fallen human tendency is to discredit or devalue yesterday because of the errors of a man or movement rather than recognize the glory there and extract it for the current generation. But this only reveals that we have not yet cultivated honor by which to perceive the great value of that glory. Honor trains us to find the eternal value our fathers and mothers possessed because their lives, even in obscure ways, pointed to and revealed the nature, character, and attributes of God. However, when we do find glory that is ours to inherit, we also find that it comes with an obligation to use it, for those who enshrine the successes and greatness of their fathers without seeking to emulate them do not honor them. We must become those who know how to receive our inheritance and use it to increase the glory passed to the next generation, setting them up to run even further and faster.

If you remember, Christ is called both the Son of God and the Everlasting Father, and we see this expressed in the way He also stood in the position of a middle generation, linking the Old and New Covenant. He didn't cast aside the Law; He fulfilled it and glorified it, and passed that glory—the revelation of the power of sin and our need for salvation—on to us. Then as a Father, He prophesied that we would take what He had given us and do *"greater works"* (John 14:12). Christ established a pattern of generational advancement for His Church, the pattern of honoring past glory, using it to build present glory, and passing it to our children to increase it further. It is the only pattern by which we will succeed in fulfilling our governmental commission. This is one application of Paul's statement:

> *According to the grace of God which was given to me, like a wise master builder I laid a foundation, and another is building on it. But each man must be careful how he builds on it. For no man can lay a foundation other than the one which is laid, which is Jesus Christ* (1 Corinthians 3:10-11).

Christ's government is called to carry His generational heart and instill it in the hearts of His Body so that we will continue to build on His foundation.

Fathering Nations

When Jesus told His disciples of His return in the Parable of the Sheep and Goats, He said that He would come *"in His glory, and all the angels with*

Him, [and] *He will sit on His glorious throne"* (Matt. 25:31). This is quite an image! All expressions of God and His attributes, power, and nature will be on display. Nothing will be hidden. The faith and hope we needed in order to see glory on Earth will no longer be required. And in this moment, Jesus says, He will divide and judge the nations according to these simple criteria:

> *For I was hungry, and you gave Me something to eat; I was thirsty, and you gave Me something to drink; I was a stranger, and you invited Me in; naked, and you clothed Me; I was sick, and you visited Me; I was in prison, and you came to Me.... Truly I say to you, to the extent that you did it to one of these brothers of Mine, even the least of them, you did it to Me* (Matthew 25:35-36,40).

This speaks to how the nations treat Christ's disciples and how they will be judged according to their response to messengers of the Gospel. But remember, Jesus was not telling this parable to the nations, but to His disciples, who He would later commission to disciple the nations. He was entrusting us with a powerful, prophetic portrait about God's expectation of the nations concerning the treatment of their most precious resource—people. Do the nations demonstrate that they see the glory of God in their people, in one another? In particular, do they practically provide for their basic human needs, including food, water, warmth, health, and freedom? Did honor flow to the least in a tangible manner?

When the Son of Man returns, He hopes to find nations who have been discipled by the Church in the goodness of God, demonstrated in that they cared for the lives of their citizens, particularly the most helpless and those who have forfeited many of their rights (prisoners). It's as if He said to us, His disciples, "They don't know it yet, but everything they do for their citizens, they are doing to Me. They are going to find out on that final day that the way they loved their poor, sick, hungry, imprisoned, and naked neighbors—or failed to—will be fully displayed before them. Your job, as My disciples, is to disciple the nations and prepare them for their final test. As My brothers, you must teach them to find the glory in all men."

Over the last 100 years or so in the Western Church, we've focused much on getting "decisions for Christ" as the primary means for making disciples. Personal confession of faith in Christ is a clear biblical principle, which I don't wish to diminish. But we can't ignore these stark criteria by which Christ says He will judge the nations He commissioned us to disciple. Whatever else we are doing, we are not discipling nations unless we are teaching them to recognize the presence of Christ in all people, especially *"the least,"* by meeting their basic human needs. Christ has called His governors to lead the nations toward Heaven's system of values by teaching them to help the helpless.

And as in all things, we must lead by example. In order to teach the nations to see and love Christ in the least, we must learn to see and love Him in the least. In order to become fathers who can lead the nations to treat men like Christ's brothers and sisters, we must first treat them like our brothers and sisters. We must put ourselves to the test the nations will face in the end: "Can I recognize Christ in someone in need? Can I see the lost, the broken, the poor, and the criminal as His family? Can I, by faith and obedience, see and honor His glory in the least long before He puts it on display for everyone to see?" The same test of honor we must pass with the generations is the test we must pass with the nations—we must become those who see the hidden gold in human lives. But whereas life flows *to* us when we honor our fathers and mothers, life flows *through* us when we honor the least.

Wherever we give life, we give hope, and hope is one of the most powerful forces in the universe. The Book of Job says, "[God] *saves…the poor from the hand of the mighty. So the helpless has hope, and unrighteousness must shut its mouth"* (Job 5:15-16). I have a childlike enjoyment in hearing the Bible tell something to shut its mouth, but beyond that, I believe this verse is describing a cause and effect. The helpless are victims of unrighteousness. But when they are given hope, the unrighteousness that brought them to their plight is silenced by that hope. One of the moms at Bethel, Olivia Shupe, gave Kris Vallotton a great phrase: "He who gives the most hope has the most influence!" In the context of the verse from Job, I think that we can begin to see why this is true. If the hope we give silences the influence of unrighteousness, then it makes room for the influence of righteousness. And, as Proverbs says, *"When it goes well with the righteous, the city rejoices..."* and *"Righteousness exalts a nation..."* (Prov. 11:10; 14:34). The giving of hope is a powerful key to the transformation of cities and nations, for it makes way for the expression of righteousness.

I appreciate an insight Bill Johnson often shares, which shows that Christ has set us up for success in our assignment to disciple nations. He reminds us that one of the prophetic names for Christ is "The Desire of All Nations": *"and I will shake all nations, and they shall come to the Desire of All Nations, and I will fill this temple with glory,' says the Lord of hosts"* (Hag. 2:7 NKJV). Then he reminds us that we are the temple in which Christ, the hope of glory, dwells, and puts this together with the Great Commission. Christ is who the nations long for, and we, who are called to teach them to recognize and embrace Him as the true object of their desire (even hidden as He is in the poorest among us), carry Him with us wherever we go. Thus, we have a power to attract them to the thing that will bring them into an eternal Kingdom, even though it is not something that is immediately attractive. This is an extraordinary thought, and it ought to give us confidence that addressing ourselves to the poor and needy instead of the rich and powerful (that subversive wisdom of the Kingdom) will ultimately prove irresistible.

One of the important lessons we must take from the Parable of the Sheep and the Goats is that people can be serving Christ's agenda and giving Him glory without consciously realizing it. We are surrounded by a culture that has inherited so many values from Christianity without knowing that they are Christian. Sir Winston Churchill, Britain's great wartime prime minister, said that you can judge the state of a civilization by the way it treats its prisoners.[3] He was speaking directly from Christ's standard. It is, of course, possible that he knew this, but it's also quite possible that he realized this simply as an inheritor of a truth that has had a long history in Britain—the standard of honor demanding that even our enemies be treated as men. There are thousands of other examples we can find around us, and we must look for them. Many of the commands of Christ we are called to teach to the nations are commands that don't require explicit acknowledgment of Christ to be obeyed. Many of these commands are already commonly accepted in our culture. We must find these points of agreement and use them as our starting points to keep building the foundation of Heaven's government in the nations. We might get further by giving our attention to these areas, where people are already serving the poor and working for justice, for example, and encouraging them, rather than focusing on how popular the name of Christ is in political polls.

I recently met a lady who has made it her life mission to end world poverty. As I heard her share, I realized that she is perhaps one of the few who has grasped the full depth of the Great Commission. She is working to get the nations ready for Jesus to examine their treatment of humanity's basic needs. I myself am currently on a steep learning curve as I wrestle with issues of social care and the most biblical model of government. According to God's economic principles, everyone is to be blessed. He has given us the ability to make wealth (see Deut. 8:18) in order that all may have provision, not to create a divide of haves and have-nots!

Third World nations are not God's idea. What is His idea is His family, and it is our job to show the poor and broken that their hope and desire has come at last. Our God will continue to be the God who rescues the poor from the mighty, but He will do it through us, His family and appointed government on the planet. He has put the Desire of the Nations within us and will draw all nations to Himself through us as we honor His glory in the least and treat them as brothers and sisters.

We have 2,000 years of an increasing inheritance of glory and momentum of discipleship with which to work in our generation. At Bethel, these truths have convinced us that we cannot fail in our commission, and we are running with passion to give hope to our city and nation. Who knows? If we can teach a nation to care for the least, then the rest may very well take care of itself.

Endnotes

1. Blue Letter Bible, "Dictionary and Word Search for *kybernēsis (Strong's 2941),*" Blue Letter Bible 1996-2011, http://www. blueletterbible.org/lang/lexicon/lexicon.cfm?strongs=G2941; accessed January 31, 2011.

2. *Thoughts on Government,* "The Originals" series (Hayes Barton Press), 2, http://books.google.com/books?id=zzV2lEgeULcC&pri ntsec=frontcover&dq=john+adams+thoughts+on+government&hl =en&ei=gRdHTYPqLo-CsQOEubDUCg&sa=X&oi=book_resul t&ct=result&resnum=1&ved=0CDQQ6AEwAA#v=snippet&q=b est%20form&f=false; accessed January 31, 2011.

3. Winston S. Churchill, *The Second World War, Volume 5: Closing the Ring* (Mariner Books, 1986), 635.

Chapter 16

OPPORTUNITIES FOR GLORY

It will lead to an opportunity for your testimony (Luke 21:13).

WHEN Christ heard that Lazarus was ill, He announced, *"This sickness is not unto death, but for the glory of God, that the Son of God may be glorified through it"* (John 11:4 NKJV). What was He saying? Well, one thing He was not saying was that God had made Lazarus sick. If there's no sickness in Heaven, He can't send it here! God is not the author of brokenness in the world. He is the author of restoration, and whenever He enters into an area of brokenness, He restores it to its original created order and purpose. This is what Christ had been revealing all along in His ministry before He made this statement. He had systematically been turning every definition, name, and limit on its head by demonstrating the dramatic reversals of God's restoration. When He came on the scene, water was no longer water, but wine; five loaves were no longer five, but thousands; storms ceased storming; the blind, lame, and leprous became otherwise; and sinners stopped sinning. When Christ said *"this sickness is not unto death,"* He was preparing His disciples to witness yet another reversal, for Lazarus, in fact, did die—only to find when Christ called him forth that death was no longer irreversible.

Christ chose the people of Israel as His audience for all of these signs because their history had trained them to recognize the glory of God—the way He expresses Himself. Those who witnessed Christ's miracles, such as the man He healed who had been born blind, knew immediately He was doing the things that only God could do:

> Since the beginning of time it has never been heard that anyone opened the eyes of a person born blind. If this man were not from God, He could do nothing (John 9:32-33).

This is the relationship Jesus was drawing their attention to when He said, "This...is...for the glory of God, that the Son of God may be glorified..." (John 11:4 NKJV). The Son of God was glorified by the opportunity to express the glory of God, for as He did so, it became increasingly apparent that God's glory was also His glory, that He truly was "the image of the invisible God," the "radiance of [the Father's] glory and the exact representation of His nature" (Col. 1:15; Heb. 1:3).

This likeness between the Son and His Father creates something of a paradox: Jesus was Himself by being like His Father. But this is just what He came to reveal to us about the nature of glory, particularly the glory He came to give to the human race. Everything God made has its own glory, which it reveals by being itself, and in being itself it is being like the One who made it. The whole universe was made to share in this pattern of the reflection between the Father, Son, and Spirit. But the human race alone in all the universe has been chosen first to be God's image-bearers and second to be His sons and daughters in Christ, "His body, the fullness of Him who fills all in all" (Eph. 1:23). Thus, in coming as the Son of God and displaying the Father's glory, Christ not only revealed Himself to be God but also revealed Himself to be Man. His greatest reversal was redefining forever what "being ourselves" meant for humanity. Just as He was Himself by being like His Father, so do we become our true selves by becoming like Him. We are glorified—our glory is expressed—by reflecting His glory. I said in the first chapter that glory is God's expression, but when Christ's restoration is complete in us, we will be able to say that glory is also our expression. This is the consummation toward which we are moving as we learn to imitate Christ just as He imitated His Father, by learning to say what He says and do what He does.

One of my chief reasons for writing this book is to bring more definition to the nature of glory, whilst also liberating glory from the confines of church buildings, Heaven in the future, or any of the other limits we like to put on it. Particularly in revival circles, there's a common association that one definition of "glory" is "something" that "shows up" at a church meeting. (Don't get me wrong—I do want to be in the room when that happens!) But there was nothing vague about the way Christ revealed His glory, and He certainly did not limit His opportunities to reveal it to the Temple or the synagogue. Everywhere He went—weddings, funerals, fishing trips, dinner parties, towns, homes, marketplaces, or the countryside—He found opportunities to express His true identity, to reveal glory. In the same way, every aspect and arena of our lives present us with opportunities to discover or reveal glory—with opportunities to be ourselves, and in being ourselves to reveal God by the way we reflect Him.

In order to recognize and step into these opportunities, however, we must continually be willing to surrender our limited ideas about who we are and look to Christ to tell us who we are. This is the formula He gave us: *"For whoever wishes to save his life will lose it; but whoever loses his life for My sake will find it"* (Matt. 16:25). He promises that as we surrender the life He gave us in the first place, He will show us how we were meant to live it. This is the journey of faith—trusting His Word above ours when it comes to who we are and how to live. It is difficult at first, when most of what we can see is what we are giving up. But as we truly begin to believe what Christ says about us and walk in it, the more we begin to experience life as we were made to live it and the thought of holding on to our old fears and small dreams becomes absurd. The life He offers us, the life we were made for, is truly abundant.

The Sermon on the Mount is Christ's manifesto calling us to become our true selves in Him, and its words provide a high-water mark for measuring where we are in "losing our lives for His sake" and finding them in Him. Consider the statement at the end of Matthew 5:

> But I say to you, love your enemies and pray for those who persecute you, so that you may be sons of your Father who is in heaven; for He causes His sun to rise on the evil and the good, and sends rain on the righteous and the unrighteous. For if you love those who love you, what reward do you have? Do not even the tax collectors do the same? If you greet only your brothers, what more are you doing than others? Do not even the Gentiles do the same? Therefore you are to be perfect, as your heavenly Father is perfect (Matthew 5:44-48).

What goes through your mind and heart when you read this command? Does the word *perfect* sound impossible or unattainable? Or are you confident that perfect is exactly where Christ is taking you, teaching and enabling you to love as a true son or daughter of the Father, just as He does? If the latter, then you are well on your way to "finding your life" in Christ. C.S. Lewis explains:

> The command *Be ye perfect* is not idealistic gas. Nor is it a command to do the impossible. He is going to make us into creatures that can obey that command. He said (in the Bible) that we were 'gods' and He is going to make good His words. If we let Him—for we can prevent Him, if we choose—he will make the feeblest and filthiest of us into a god or goddess, a dazzling, radiant, immortal creature, pulsating all through with such energy and joy and wisdom and love as we cannot now imagine, a bright stainless mirror which reflects back to God perfectly (though, of course,

on a smaller scale) His own boundless power and delight and goodness. The process will be long and in parts very painful, but that is what we are in for. Nothing less. He meant what He said. Just try to imagine what it will mean for you and me and the whole Body of Christ to become perfect reflections of God in our words, our thoughts, our character, and our relationships. It is unfathomable, but it will happen, and every moment of our lives is an opportunity to move toward it.[1]

Being Ourselves

I am so glad to live in a generation in the Church that is realizing that standing behind a pulpit is not the only spiritual calling. When we became Christ's, He did not separate our lives into sacred and secular. He has not commissioned us merely to hold meetings and services but to bring Heaven to Earth, *"Every place on which the* [soles of our feet tread]" (Josh. 1:3). All that we are is sacred if we belong to Him, every aspect of our lives is designed to express glory, and the highest calling for each of us is to manifest His glory in whatever arena He has designed us to serve. Some of us will do this in a pulpit, but others may do it on the catwalk at a fashion show, in an art or music studio, in a university classroom, or in a medical laboratory dedicated to discovering a cure for cancer. In fact, most of us will be doing it anywhere but in a pulpit!

This revelation, that in the Kingdom every aspect of our lives was designed to reflect and express glory, is extremely liberating. It opens the field wide for us to dream with God and believe that, though He has made us all one Body with a common purpose, each of us has something unique and important to creatively contribute. After all, we were made in the image of the Creator to be creative! Instead of being made to fit a certain mold, we are made to freely discover who He made us to be through the exchange of relationship with Him, by which He awakens our hearts and stirs our desires for the things He made us to do. And when our assignments flow out of this partnership and passion, they do not feel like duties or heavy burdens. There is nothing that will give us satisfaction, pleasure, and energy like being and doing what God dreamed us up to be and to do.

Yet, in the chapter on beauty, I described how the things we find beautiful and the way they attract us will bring to the surface God's unique design and call in each of our lives. I recently spoke to a photography class on this subject of beauty, and the following day I received this testimony:

> I just wanted to let you know what a blessing and influence your talk was today. I am not exaggerating when I say that today was a milestone that I will remember for the rest of my days. What a word in season, and how powerfully, or should I say "beautifully," expressed!

> Could I give you a little background? From my very first thought about what I wanted to do vocationally, I have only had one desire. I was interviewed at a family Christmas gathering when I was 10 years old, and I have on video my answer to my uncle asking me what I wanted to be when I grew up. "I want to be a television cameraman," was my answer.

> Schoolteachers and pastors have sometimes tried to open up my options, because I have had such a single-minded vision for my future. But no matter what they said, and no matter how much I tried to take on board what they were telling me, I couldn't do it. I was, and continue to believe that I was, born to do what I do, and going against it is denying who I am.

I have realized my dream as a cameraman and am currently on sabbatical from a large production studio. In the TV world, it doesn't get any better than this. I have also had an equally strong desire grow in me over the last three to four years to go into full-time ministry and so have been trying to find out what that looks like. I've been in leadership in my home church and have explored and served in many different ways but have never put my most fundamental joy and gift into the ministry mix. It never occurred to me that God had a plan to marry all these different desires into one.

Today, the penny dropped. I had been trying to find and fit myself into a ministry mould that best suit me. I was having some success but nothing like today. As you spoke this afternoon, the Lord showed me that my ministry and my heart's desire are one and the same thing! It may seem so obvious to an onlooker, but I just couldn't see it, because what I was looking for wasn't being modeled by anyone I knew of. I felt the permission and commission from Heaven to pursue the outworking of what I found beautiful.

What release and freedom! Thank you so much for opening my eyes to the call to pursue the gifts God has placed in our lives, with the view to transforming the world. This is not a substitute for the fivefold ministry. It's the real deal and the ultimate call on our lives. I have been volunteering with the media department, absolutely loving every minute of it, but deep down thinking that one day, the time will come for me to move into "recognized" ministry. No! What is before me at the moment is the outworking of the rest of my life. Whether I am at Bethel or not (subject to visas), I will forever burn for Jesus through film!

I feel like today was the first day of the rest of my life. I will forever be grateful for your word of release to me. We may have been quiet in class, but my whole world rocked today!

I know there are many believers who, like this man, have struggled to reconcile their heart's desire to pursue a certain career or project with their desire to serve and glorify God. They think that glorifying Him means they must sacrifice or diminish the things that are most personal and unique about them. But this is not how God's glory works. If we truly desire to reflect God's glory and surrender ourselves to God, then God is going to bring the unique ways He designed us to reflect Him to the surface in each one of us. My hope and prayer is that every believer on the planet receives Heaven's permission, as this man did, to run after the things God put in their hearts and not continue waiting for a "real" ministry or compartmentalizing their lives into ministry, career, family, etc. Such hesitation and division only hinder our freedom and momentum, thereby robbing the world of benefiting from the full potential of our gifts and robbing us of the full measure of joy God wants us to receive by doing what we were made to do.

Being Like Him

I remind you of the connection between glory and joy, the connection expressed so well in the Westminster Catechism that our "chief purpose is to glorify God and enjoy Him forever."[2] The two things are not separate. The deepest joy God can give us is the joy we experience in glorifying Him by being who He made us to be in relationship with Him. Experiencing this joy, as we read in the above testimony, is like a homecoming—we begin to feel we belong here as we see the glorious pattern God is weaving from the seemingly disparate threads in our lives. None of us will know this joy fully in this life, for our true homecoming lies beyond it. But we can begin to feel the joy of drawing near to it.

If we look closer at the joy of becoming our true selves in God, however, we find that in fact it is His joy, for in reflecting Him, we please Him, and there is no greater joy than the pleasure and delight of God. This was the joy Scottish runner and missionary Eric Liddell experienced. In the 1981 film *Chariots of Fire*, Liddell's character says, "I believe that God made me for a purpose but He also made me fast. When I run, I feel His pleasure."[3] And this was the joy C.S. Lewis specifically described as the fulfillment of the "promise of glory":

> No one can enter heaven except as a child; and nothing is so obvious in a child—not in a conceited child, but in a good child—as its great and undisguised pleasure in being praised... The promise of glory is the promise, almost incredible and only possibly by the work of Christ, that some of us, that any of us who really chooses...shall find approval, shall please God. To please God...to be a real ingredient in the divine happiness...to be loved by God, not merely pitied, but delighted in as an artist delights in his work or a father his son—it seems impossible, a weight or burden of glory which our thoughts can hardly sustain. But so it is.[4]

One of the greatest moments of this joy recorded in the Gospels occurred when Jesus' disciples returned from their first ministry trip. He had sent them out as His spiritual sons, anointing and authorizing them to fully represent Him in preaching and in performing signs and wonders. This was the first time they got to experience in some measure what it was like to be Him, and it was exhilarating:

> *The seventy returned with joy, saying, "Lord, even the demons are subject to us in Your name."... At that very time He rejoiced*

greatly in the Holy Spirit, and said, "I praise You, O Father, Lord of heaven and earth, that You have hidden these things from the wise and intelligent and have revealed them to infants. Yes, Father, for this way was well-pleasing in Your sight" (Luke 10:17,21).

I would have loved to see Jesus "rejoice greatly in the Holy Spirit." He had the double joy of a father and son. As a father, He had the joy of seeing His spiritual sons step more fully into their calling and identity, and as a fellow son, He had the joy of knowing that they now shared the incredible joy He knew as a Son in doing the will of His Father. This multiplied joy of God is what we are destined to share as we learn to reflect Him.

In the summer of 2005, my son James gave me one of the greatest revelations, a revelation I had never seen before, about the joy we were made to experience as sons and daughters of our Father. It was particularly significant to me because I had only begun my return to sonship just weeks before. I know every preacher uses family illustrations to make a point, but this wasn't just personal; it really was an entirely new concept to me. Because his experience was so profound for both of us, I asked my son James to write about it for this book. (I include it for that reason but also because I wanted three generations of Manwarings to contribute to this book!)

It was a Thursday in July when James called me, more excited than I had heard him in a long time. Even living apart, we have many great conversations about life, movies, Apple computers, cameras, and our walks with God. We are so grateful for modern technology that enables our regular communication. But this conversation was different. He wanted to tell me of the events that had taken place at the Salvation Army music school he had been helping to lead. James is a musician with a passion for people. I often describe him to people as a mixture of three of his favorite movies: *Mr. Holland's Opus*, *Good Will Hunting*, and *Dead Poets Society*. Wherever James is, there will be people and music. This is what he told me and later wrote:

I'm not sure about you, but I am someone who has several heroes, people I look at and look to. Heroes come from all different backgrounds and gain status for a number of different reasons. I have grown up with heroes, such as pianist Jools Holland, composer Rachmaninoff, and speaker and writer Billy Graham, to name just a few. However, as you grow up things change, and new heroes come along and sometimes replace the old ones.

One of my heroes is a fictional character from a film called *Mr. Holland's Opus*. Mr. Holland is the most inspirational music teacher I have known and yet never met. When I first saw the film, something switched inside me, and I wanted to emulate him. Now I have the privilege of teaching music every day of my life. Having the chance to live out the dream that was created through watching that film is amazing, and I thank God for His grace and provision for me and my career.

Another hero is, of course, my own father. As I have grown up, I have learned that above all, the greatest hero that one can have is a dad, and I have two! What better feeling than to feel like you are walking in the footsteps of your greatest hero? That is surely the goal, to feel like you have done something heroic that fits in with what they stand for. It was in the summer of 2005 that I felt I stepped into a new phase in my spiritual life, where I gained this life-changing revelation about fatherhood and a feeling that I can only try and explain in these coming lines.

I was attending a youth summer camp where God had really been showing up. The Lord was moving in a powerful way, and I could really feel the presence of God falling on people's lives. The young people were being changed, renewed by the power of God, and I was right there in the center of it, leading them into new dreams and visions for their lives. It was in one of these amazing and powerful moments that I really began to minister. I began to speak into people's lives. I began to declare over the lives of the young people what I believe God wanted for each and every one of them. It was intense, exciting, and altogether God and good. I really felt empowered by the Spirit and excited about what the Lord was doing for these young people.

It was in this moment that I truly felt like my dad. I felt that I was walking as he would in that situation. I felt like I was him. I called Dad in the United States from the United Kingdom and didn't really say much; I simply said, "I felt like you, Dad." It was in that moment that this distinctly simple phrase was born into our family. It's a phrase that, on the surface, sounds like something nice you would write on a postcard home, but actually is a deep message that I have sought to live out—what is it to truly feel like our Father in Heaven? Can we experience the same feeling that Jesus felt as He walked on this earth? I am sure that if He had had an iPhone, He would have called up God and said, "Hey, Dad, I felt like You today in the village when that blind guy got his sight back."

Since that day, I have wanted to try and live out this message. If we can seek to feel like our Father in Heaven and seek to live out His life on Earth as one of our greatest heroes, then God can start to change lives. The message for me was also that it mattered that I had a dad and it was so important that I felt like him, that I modeled myself on him and recognized when I was walking in his footsteps. And that takes me back to the heroes thing. If your hero is a famous singer, then you want nothing more than to sing just like him and therefore feel like he does when he sings. And so for me, my greatest heroes are my two fathers, one on Earth and one in Heaven. I seek to feel like them because I want to live my life in line with what they believe. Having a hero is a good thing—well, I guess the right sort of hero—but you get my point. Having God the Father as your hero is definitely the way to go, and seeking to feel like Jesus did on Earth when He was living out the true messages of God's love is to seek to feel like your Father in Heaven. And so I felt like you, Dad, and even as I write this now, I feel like my dad, sitting at my MacBook, writing something…I am sure he has done something similar this week.

Five thousand six hundred miles away, I greatly enjoyed hearing my son's testimony of stepping out in ministry. But when he got to the end and said, "I felt like you, Dad," my eyes filled with tears—tears of pride and joy in my son, but also tears of being overwhelmed by this fresh revelation. It made perfect sense that this was the same feeling that motivated Christ, for what else could be behind His commitment to do only what the Father did than His great joy in feeling like His Dad?! He said that being like His Dad, doing what His Dad did, was the "food" that sustained and nourished Him (see John 4:34). But it was amazing to realize that even as Christ experienced this incredible feeling of being like His Dad, He was promising the same sustenance, thrill, and delight to us. As we travel our own journey from glory to glory, we have a Father in Heaven waiting for us, as we lay hands on the sick, feed the hungry, paint or express ourselves creatively, or otherwise do what He does, to say, "When I did that, I felt like You, Dad. I was the reflection of Your glory here on Earth."

The key to entering into this promise, as James said, is learning to see our heavenly Father and Christ as heroes, as the ones we most want to be like and to please. This is why it is so important for us to receive healing from all father wounds and misaligned relationships and embrace the mind and heart of sonship. Until we do, we won't perceive the Father's instruction for being like Him for what it is—His invitation to experience the greatest joy and satisfaction He can possibly give us.

The Greater Realities

At Bethel, we gratefully acknowledge the spiritual inheritance we've received from courageous men and women who have contended for the birthright of every son and daughter of God to reflect and manifest the glory of their Father, just as our Elder Brother did, particularly in the area of supernatural ministry. It is revolutionary in any generation to affirm that Christ was showing us how to be human when He ministered with supernatural power, but we believe this is the revolution He began, and we are aligning ourselves with those who have carried this message. John Wimber is one of these spiritual fathers—he used to say that we get to "do the stuff" Jesus did, the supernatural. I am amazed to see the results that have come and continue to come as the men and women in our School of Ministry run with this message. They find opportunities to display the glory of a supernatural God in every store and street in town, and their testimonies of how He shows up in power have created an overwhelming tide of evidence supporting His promise that signs and wonders truly do follow those who believe (see Mark 16:17).

But signs, as Bill Johnson often points out, are not ultimate realities. They point to ultimate realities, and if we don't follow the signs to these ultimate realities, then we have not received the full benefit of the sign. What is the full benefit of the gift of healing, for example? I know well that it is one of the greatest privileges to lay hands on the sick and see them healed. Having trained and worked as a nurse, I have often watched helplessly as patients were told that there was nothing that could be done for their illnesses. And as a minister, I have seen the dramatic difference it makes when we carry the presence of the One who *"heals all* [our] *diseases"* (Ps. 103:3) into the room. The obvious benefit is that a person receives restoration in his or her body, and anyone who has received this restoration knows this is incredible! But there is an even greater benefit that the healing has to offer: the revelation of the God who heals. This revelation is an invitation for the person to know Him as the Healer and to become a carrier of that revelation to the world. That is the glory of healing.

The same thing is true of the other gifts of the Spirit. I once was leading a meeting in Texas. At the beginning of the meeting, I saw, in my mind's eye, a stop sign and a violin. I stood up, described the vision, and asked the congregation, "Does this mean anything to anybody?" A lady immediately responded, "Ten years ago, I was in a car accident and I damaged my neck. Up until then I'd been a violinist on a worship team, and ever since I've not been able to play the violin." At the meeting she got 75 percent healed. We went after her healing a bit more but couldn't get the last 25 percent. Finally, I looked at her and said, "I've got a feeling that when you pick up your violin, you'll get fully healed." She went home and picked up her violin. The next night she came back to the meeting and played her violin for two nights.

This word of knowledge led to the obvious benefit of healing for this lady. But it did more—it revealed God's deep affection for and interest in her, as well as His plan and purpose for her life and invited her to step toward them. Significantly, she couldn't receive the full benefit of the word until she responded to that invitation. And because she did, the glory of that gift continues to be revealed every time she plays her violin on the worship team, inviting others to know the God who loves them and desires to restore them to their glory in the same way.

God's acts reveal His ways and lead us to know Him, if we follow the signs to these ultimate realities. And it is only by coming to know Him, by gaining *yada*, that we become those who can reflect and reveal God's character through our own acts. We see this clearly with Moses. Remember, Israel knew God's acts, but Moses knew God's ways (see Ps. 103:7). Only Moses pressed in for *yada* of God's glory, and this is why God made Moses His representative. This relational knowledge, this revelation of God's glory and how it works, is what God made us to live from. This is why, for example, the Bible doesn't only give us the command, *"Forgive, and you will be forgiven"* (Luke 6:37 NKJV). It also says, *"The discretion of a man makes him slow to anger, and his glory is to overlook a transgression"* (Prov. 19:11 NKJV) and then tells the story of the Man who was glorified by forgiving the transgression of the entire world, the Man who turned to those He had forgiven and said, *"If you forgive the sins of any, their sins have been forgiven them"* (John 20:23).

Forgiveness is the privilege and assignment of the royalty of Heaven. I don't know about you, but I think our ability to forgive is greatly enhanced by knowing that every time we cover another's transgression, we are walking as true sons of our Father by carrying out the family business of forgiveness. We begin to recognize seeing another's transgression as an opportunity, living as we do in a culture that revels in exposing and judging people's faults and failures, to partner with Christ in creating yet another one of Heaven's dramatic reversals.

I share the passion of my brothers and sisters at Bethel to pursue the miraculous; for me this passion flows from my desire that the Body truly becomes the expression of Christ, the reflection of the Father, in everything. I believe, in fact, that not just miracles but everything we do, from playing with our children to paying the bills, writing a song, arranging a business deal, going to war, or calling a friend can be supernatural, can be glorious, for they have the potential to reflect aspects of God's nature. I'm convinced that if we look for and discover the glory in these things, we will not do them the same way we've always done them. They will be infused with purpose and consecration, with passion and joy, and these attributes always produce excellence. Ultimately, as we find and take the opportunities for glory around us, we will, as Christ did, put human life as it was meant to be lived on display for the world to see. And like Christ, we will be able to say with absolute truth, "If you have seen us, you have seen the Father."

Endnotes

1. C. S. Lewis, *Mere Christianity* (New York, NY; Harper Collins, 1953), 173-74.

2. James R. Boyd, *The Westminster Shorter Catechism* (Philadelphia: Presbyterian Board of Publication, 1854), 19, http://books.google. com/books?id=vyFMAAAAYAAJ&printsec=frontcover&dq=west minster+catechism&hl=en&ei=7tZETZsbi6KwA6LYhZMK&sa =X&oi=book_result&ct=result&resnum=1&ved=0CC4Q6AEwA A#v=onepage&q&f=false; accessed January 29, 2011.

3. Peter E. Dans, *Christians in the Movies: A Century of Saints and Sinners* (Lanham, MD: Rowman & Littlefield Publishers, Inc., 2009), 222.

4. C.S. Lewis, *Essay Collection and Other Short Pieces* (London: Harper Collins, 2000), 101-2.

Chapter 17

NOTHING BUT GLORY

And the city has no need of the sun or of the moon to shine on it,
for the glory of God has illumined it, and its lamp is the Lamb
(Revelation 21:23).

THE World and all who inhabit it are waiting for the earth to be filled with the knowledge of the glory of the Lord. They are waiting for Heaven on Earth. As I have pointed out a few times throughout this book, our thinking shifts dramatically when we understand that Heaven is not simply a future reality but an eternal one, which includes the present. It is the eternal reality upon which Paul instructed us to "set our minds" (see Col. 3:2) or in the King James Version, "*set* [our] *affection*" (Col. 3:2). We are to train our desires to love and long for that superior reality, for our desire is the fuel that drives us to become the "*violent*" ones who "*take* [the kingdom of heaven] *by force*" and bring it to earth (Matt. 11:12).

Training our minds and affections on Heaven involves training our imaginations. This is no easy task, for technically it is beyond our conception, as life outside the womb is beyond the conception of a fetus. As Scripture says, "*Beloved, now we are children of God, and it has not appeared as yet what we will be*" (1 John 3:2). To begin to imagine how unimaginable Heaven is, just try explaining to a caveman the wonders of modern transport or even to Ansel Adams the world of digital photography. I myself have found religious teaching that takes the Bible's descriptions literally and paints Heaven as a cathedral in the sky less than inviting. But in studying the nature of glory, my imagination has been freed. As I have looked back at the Bible's descriptions of Heaven, knowing that all I've learned of glory derives from that reality, these accounts have opened up to me in a new way.

For example, John's visions describe Heaven as a city made of crystal, gold, and precious stones (see Rev. 4:6; 21:18). This image finally made sense when I learned about the reflective nature of glory, for all of those materials either reflect (crystal and gold) or refract (precious stones). This is a beautiful image of the principle we saw in the last chapter, that everything in the universe, particularly the human race made in His image, is made to reflect God. Refraction is multiplied reflection, another aspect seen in all of creation but especially in the human race, for we were commanded to multiply and fill the earth with the glorious image of God.

When the images of gold, jewels, and crystal made sense to me, then the meaning of another image also became clear. The picture of the four living creatures covered in eyes around the throne crying *"Holy, Holy, Holy"* (see Rev. 4:8) used to strike me as mindless repetition. But then I began to imagine what it would mean for all the glorious things I have begun to describe in this book to exist in a realm where everything is designed to reflect and refract that glory, endlessly magnifying and multiplying all that we only have the barest glimpse of here—the love, relationships, goodness, joy, beauty, creativity, and wisdom. Every nanosecond, there is a fresh unveiling of glory. No wonder the cry is "Holy, Holy, Holy!" Those watching will surely gasp and bow as another scene is unveiled. It is also no wonder that the living creatures have eyes everywhere. They will need them to glimpse all that is being unfurled, both without and within.

Probably the most powerful image of Heaven is the image of the wedding feast, the great family reunion at the restoration of all things. This image is significant because, now that I see the glory in the best of what I have tasted here on Earth, I know it can only be a hint of what we will experience in Heaven. It was a family reunion that prompted the happiest two words I had ever heard in my home, the words my son Luke shouted at the top of his voice at 6:30 one Saturday morning in May 2005: *"No way!"* (I say "had heard" because our daughter-in-law Amy may have stolen the happiest words award when she announced that she was pregnant.)

In order to put these exuberant words in context, I must go back and tell the story that led up to them; the story that began four years earlier, when Sue, Luke, and I left England and our eldest son James just four days after September 11, 2001. We were due to fly on Thursday, September 13, but the attack on the World Trade Center caused all flights to be cancelled. We were reissued tickets for three weeks later. We had our visas to live in America for a year, had sold our house, and I had left my work as a prison governor (warden) on a five-year career break. We were ready and wanting to go, though we were also conscious that others had more urgent and compassionate reasons to be on the first planes to leave for America. Despite that, Sue was relentless in contacting the airline to get the most up-to-date information on an almost hour-by-hour basis.

On September 15, she was informed that a window in the closed skies between London and San Francisco had opened. Without the notice that our original plans had allowed, we bundled into my son's car and hurriedly left for Heathrow Airport, not knowing if we would get on a plane that day or spend days camped out at the airport. To this day, we do not know how we managed to say good-bye to James at the side of the road at Heathrow, or how he had the courage to pursue his future while his parents and brother followed a call to go to America. (Thank you so much, James, for your sacrifice in letting us go and, more than that, for your constant encouragement.) It was truthfully an experience of God's *empowering presence*, which has for a long time been my favorite description of God's grace. Miraculously, we did get on the only plane that flew from Heathrow to San Francisco that day, and so began our new life in the United States of America.

Since then, we have learned to live several thousand miles away from our eldest son, and now away from his wife and our first grandson. We have learned to use and be daily grateful for the modern-day miracle of email and instant messaging, and for this reminder that we only live apart, and have not lost our son, as some of our dear friends have. Nonetheless, there is an absence in our home, a separation that reminds us of the price of pursuing God's call. I myself made my first commitment to that call when I was aged 18, in the words of Dr. David Livingstone:

> Lord, send me anywhere, only go with me. Lay any burden on me, only sustain me. Sever any ties, save the tie that binds me to Thy heart.[1]

Little did I know how fully I would live out that prayer. But I do know fully that God has kept His part of the prayer.

James visited us many times in Redding after we moved there, but in May 2005, I had the opportunity of arranging a surprise visit. It was great fun to plan this with him and to talk to him on the phone as he sat in a plane at Heathrow telling his mother he was going to visit London during his school vacation. With complex subterfuge, I brought Sue to meet James at the Sacramento airport, where she had a wonderful surprise reunion. But far more fun was the reunion with his brother Luke. That night, Luke was at a "sobergrad" party as the guest of a graduate, which I had not planned. This meant that he spent the whole night out and returned home early in the morning. At 6:30 A.M., we heard the garage door open and a tired young man stagger into his bedroom, only to be greeted by his brother, who had slept in his bed. The joy was evident for us—and perhaps the neighbors! It was a moment of absolute joy as Luke shouted, *"No way!"*

This event made me aware of how God the Father has planned for all eternity to bring His family back together. If I, as a sinful earthly father, would delight in preparing such a reunion, how much more does our heavenly Father? It is easy to read the story of the Fall as the story of Adam and Eve losing relationship with God in The Garden. But God's pursuit of Adam shows us that God lost something when man first sinned. If we can begin to understand what God lost then we can begin to understand the lengths to which He has gone to restore His family, actions that culminated in the sending of and sacrificial separation from His Son Jesus. In His great prayer in John 17, Jesus makes it clear that He was in Heaven with His Father before the world was created. For me, this evokes an image of God the Father having to say good-bye to His Son. In some way, the repeated experience I have had saying good-bye to James at San Francisco Airport has given me a minute glimpse of what He must have felt being separated from Christ at the cross: *"My God, My God, why have You forsaken Me?"* (Matt. 27:46). But the answer to this cry is that God wants His kids back. He knew that the separation was worth the price to create a great heavenly reunion, a wedding celebration for His Son. And Heaven is designed for this glorious reunion. We will forever cry "Holy, Holy, Holy!"—or perhaps, *"No way!"*

Students of Glory

When we allow our imaginations to wander through these heavenly pictures, it is easy to wonder if we are merely indulging in fantasies and daydreams. The truth is that training our imaginations and desires to see and long for Heaven is one of the most practical things we can do, for the reality our hearts' affections are attached to is the reality we will create around us. As C.S. Lewis stated in *Mere Christianity*:

> A continual looking forward to the eternal world is not (as some modern people think) a form of escapism or wishful thinking, but one of the things a Christian is meant to do. It does not mean that we are to leave the present world as it is. If you read history you will find that the Christians who

did most for the present world were just those who thought most of the next. The Apostles themselves, who set on foot the conversion of the Roman Empire, the great men who built up the Middle Ages, the English Evangelicals who abolished the Slave Trade, all left their mark on Earth, precisely because their minds were occupied with Heaven. It is since Christians have largely ceased to think of the other world that they have become so ineffective in this. Aim at Heaven and you will get earth "thrown in": aim at earth and you will get neither.[2]

This book represents my journey to occupy my mind with Heaven and anchor my heart in the reality and nature of glory so that I can be effective in this life and in eternity. Significantly, this was not a journey I initiated. The subject of glory was not my idea. It happened to me, pursued me, and before I knew it, I found myself on a great adventure. Clues enticed me and demanded answers, and people encouraged my studies with their own stories and revelations.

My favorite moment in writing this book was the morning that I sat and read all of Moses' trips up and down the mountain. In my investigative style, I drew a chart of the trips. I had always thought that it was being in the physical presence of God that made Moses' face shine. Imagine my delight as I saw that it was when he was hidden in the cleft of a rock and heard God describe how good He was. Then I read on to Moses' fourth trip when he blessed those who would enter the Promised Land. I had always felt sorry for Moses. After all his boldness, faith, and commitment, one act of disobedience kept him from his destination. Yet he stood courageously and passed the baton of revival to the next generation, declaring that they would go further and have greater victories than he had. And then I saw for the first time (I am sure many others have seen this) that Moses did make it to the Promised Land.

On the Mount of Transfiguration, he joined Elijah in representing the Old Testament and met with Jesus, who would fulfill what they began and establish the New Covenant. That was his fifth trip up the mountain. For those who study numbers and their meaning, five often means grace. And that is exactly what that trip was—an act of grace by God. Moses was privileged not only to make it to the Promised Land, but also to experience one of the pinnacle moments (literally) of the New Testament. He got to see Christ glorified, the ultimate answer to his audacious request! This is such a great encouragement to all of us, especially those who perhaps have felt that they have gone around the mountain too many times. God is fully committed to finishing the glorious work He has begun in each one of us, to fulfill what He has put in our hearts and make it a blessing to the generations behind and before us, no matter how long it takes.

Recently, a man prayed for me. In his prayer, he used the word *"resign,"* but he changed the intonation and it became "re-sign." As he prayed it prophetically over me—one cancer survivor praying for another—I realized how powerful that word is when pronounced in this way. All of us have an invitation—not to resign or give up, but rather to re-sign, to re-enroll as students and seekers of glory in every circumstance, no matter how difficult or discouraging. There really always is more. My mother is a great example of this attitude for me. Today, at 87 years of age, she is a hospital chaplain and chairwoman of a Prison Fellowship that visits and ministers in a high-security women's prison in England. She has had more opportunities than most to resign. She lost her mother to tuberculosis at age four, served in the land army during the Second World War, and saw her husband die of cancer after only 21 years of marriage. But she has never resigned. In every season and every challenge, she has taken it as an opportunity to re-sign and pursue glory.

Moses' journey on Earth took him from glory to glory, and that journey did not stop when he died, but continued into eternity. I myself have purposed to follow Moses and enroll myself as a lifelong student of glory—until I graduate to the master's program, and then it will be nothing but glory! But as my own passion and interest in glory has grown, so has my passion to draw others into the journey with me, for glory is made to be shared. I am convinced by the words of Lewis in his conclusion to his sermon, "The Weight of Glory":

> It may be possible for each to think too much of his own potential glory hereafter; it is hardly possible for him to think too often or too deeply about that of his neighbour. The load, or weight, or burden of my neighbour's glory should be laid daily on my back, a load so heavy that only humility can carry it, and the backs of the proud will be broken. It is a serious thing to live in a society of possible gods and goddesses, to remember that the dullest and most uninteresting person you can talk to may one day be a creature which, if you saw it now, you would be strongly tempted to worship, or else a horror and a corruption such as you now meet, if at all, only in a nightmare. All day long we are, in some degree, helping each other to one or other of these destinations. It is in the light of these overwhelming possibilities, it is with the awe and the circumspection proper to them, that we should conduct all our dealings with one another, all friendships, all loves, all play, all politics. There are no ordinary people. You have never talked to a mere mortal. Nations, cultures, arts, civilisations—these are mortal, and their life is to ours as the life of a gnat. But it is immortals whom we joke with, work with, marry, snub, and exploit—immortal horrors or everlasting splendours.[3]

"There are no ordinary people." We are all called to an eternal journey that will take us from glory to glory and ultimately to the great cloud of witnesses, where we will watch as those who follow us continue and complete the work of revealing the fullness of God's glory in the earth, culminating in the most glorious wedding and family reunion, which will last for eternity. It is our glory as members of the eternal royal family in every generation to prepare for these events by searching out the matters God has hidden for us and helping one another become the "everlasting splendors" we were made to be. What else is waiting to be discovered? What is waiting to be created? What journeys, begun by our forefathers, are crying out to be completed? If this book has left you asking these kinds of questions, if I have in any way convinced you to enroll in the same program as a student of glory, then it will have fulfilled its purpose.

Endnotes

1. "Livingstone, David (1813-1873)," *Gospel Fellowship Association,* November 11, 2005, http://www.gfamissions.org/missionary-biographies/livingstone-david-1813-1873.html; accessed January 31, 2011.

2. C.S. Lewis, *Mere Christianity* (New York: HarperCollins, 2001), 137.

3. C.S. Lewis, *The Weight of Glory* (New York: HarperCollins, 2001), 46.

THE AFTERWORD

WE, James and Luke, felt that as the book is so much about family that we should have the last word…so here it is!

In many ways, as brothers, we couldn't be more different. One of us loves opera, reading books, and working as a teacher. The other loves football, doesn't read, and likes to work behind a video camera. And yet, we are immensely close and incredibly similar when you get to know us. And so we find ourselves writing this afterword, and despite our different approaches to reading books, we can offer a different take on the book that you have just read. And that is, of course, a look at the man behind this book—our dad.

Our dad has had an immense impact on both of our lives, and he remains, to this day, our hero. He has saved lives as a nurse, has restored lives as a prison governor, and is now changing lives as a pastor. But above all this, he has been our constant strength and has dedicated the last 27 years of his life to being our dad. Whether it is working long hours to provide food and shelter or driving us to music lessons or football training, he has always put his sons first. When we, his sons, have made important, life-changing decisions, he has backed us all the way. When we have messed up and fallen short, he picked us up.

This book was birthed out of an experience that we will both never forget. Picture the scene—one of us lives in America (Luke) and the other comes over for a surprise visit (James). Such a surprise was, for both of us, one of the happiest moments in our lives and remains one of our fondest memories.

The overwhelming love Dad has for us, as his sons, reflects the very same love God has for His children. Perhaps the best decision Dad has ever made was to marry our mum. She is the strongest, most courageous woman we have ever met, and we have the privilege of being her sons. Living on two different continents is never easy, but our parents have always made sure that we get to see each other as often as possible. Together we are unstoppable; we are the Manwarings.

Dad, if you are proud of us, it is merely our response to being raised by such an incredible man.

—James and Luke Manwaring

ABOUT PAUL MANWARING

PAUL Manwaring is a pastor and a member of the senior management team at Bethel Church. His primary responsibilities are to oversee Global Legacy, an apostolic relational network of revival leaders, and to equip and deploy revivalists through his oversight of the third year program in Bethel's School of Supernatural Ministry. Paul truly carries the gift of administration/government and releases that power and wisdom through his Supernatural Strategic Planning Workshops, his itinerant ministry, and his teaching at BSSM. His passion is to see the Bride prepared, glorious sons and daughters revealed, cancer destroyed, and cities transformed as the government of Heaven is established on Earth. After a career in senior prison management in England, Paul came to Bethel in 2001. He holds a master's degree in management from Cambridge University and is a registered general and psychiatric nurse.

Visit the Bethel Church Website at http://www.ibethel.org.

NOTES

In the right hands, This Book will Change Lives!

Most of the people who need this message will not be looking for this book. To change their lives, you need to put a copy of this book in their hands.

> *But others (seeds) fell into good ground, and brought forth fruit, some a hundred-fold, some sixty-fold, some thirty-fold* (Matthew 13:8).

Our ministry is constantly seeking methods to find the good ground, the people who need this anointed message to change their lives. Will you help us reach these people?

> *Remember this—a farmer who plants only a few seeds will get a small crop. But the one who plants generously will get a generous crop* (2 Corinthians 9:6).

EXTEND THIS MINISTRY BY SOWING
3 BOOKS, 5 BOOKS, 10 BOOKS, OR MORE TODAY,
AND BECOME A LIFE CHANGER!

Thank you,

Don Nori Sr., Founder
Destiny Image
Since 1982